WRITER-FILES

General Editor: Simon Trussler

Associate Editor: Malcolm Page

File on
BRENTON

Compiled by Tony Mitchell

Methuen. London and New York

A Methuen Paperback
First published in 1987 as a paperback original
by Methuen London Ltd,
11 New Fetter Lane, London EC4P 4EE
and Methuen Inc, 29 West 35th Street,
New York, NY 10001

Typeset in 9/10 Times
by L. Anderson Typesetting
Woodchurch, Kent TN26 3TB
Printed in Great Britain
by Richard Clay (The Chaucer Press) Ltd,
Bungay, Suffolk

British Library Cataloguing in Publication Data

Mitchell, Tony
    File on Brenton. — (Writer-files)
    1. Drama in English. Brenton, Howard,
    1942-. Critical Studies
    I. Title   II. Series
    822'.914

    ISBN 0-413-14540-9

Contents

Acknowledgements

I would like to thank Howard Brenton and
Joanna Marston of Rosica Colin, Ltd., for their
assistance in preparing this book, which was also
made possible by a Special Research Grant from
the University of New South Wales, Australia.

The theatre is, by its nature, an ephemeral art: yet it is a daunting task to track down the newspaper reviews, or contemporary statements from the writer or his director, which are often all that remain to help us recreate some sense of what a particular production was like. This series is therefore intended to make readily available a selection of the comments that the critics made about the plays of leading modern dramatists at the time of their production — and to trace, too, the course of each writer's own views about his work and his world.

In addition to combining a uniquely convenient source of such elusive *documentation*, the 'Writer-Files' series also assembles the *information* necessary for readers to pursue further their interest in a particular writer or work. Variations in quantity between one writer's output and another, differences in temperament which make some readier than others to talk about their work, and the variety of critical response, all mean that the presentation and balance of material shifts between one volume and another: but we have tried to arrive at a format for the series which will nevertheless enable users of one volume readily to find their way around any other.

Section 1, 'A Brief Chronology', provides a quick conspective overview of each playwright's life and career. *Section 2* deals with the plays themselves, arranged chronologically in the order of their composition: information on first performances, major revivals, and publication is followed by a brief synopsis (for quick reference set in slightly larger, italic type), then by a representative selection of the critical response, and of the dramatist's own comments on the play and its theme.

Section 3 offers concise guidance to each writer's work in non-dramatic forms, while *Section 4*, 'The Writer on His Work', brings together comments from the playwright himself on more general matters of construction, opinion, and artistic development. Finally, *Section 5* provides a bibliographical guide to other primary and secondary sources of further reading, among which full details will be found of works cited elsewhere under short titles, and of collected editions of the plays — but not of individual titles, particulars of which will be found with the other factual data in Section 2.

The 'Writer-Files' hope by striking this kind of balance between information and a wide range of opinion to offer 'companions' to the study of major playwrights in the modern repertoire — not in that dangerous pre-digested fashion which can too readily quench the desire to read the plays themselves, nor so prescriptively as to allow any single line of approach to predominate, but rather to encourage readers to form their own judgements of the plays in a wide-ranging context.

Howard Brenton, of all the dramatists of his generation, seems to arouse the fiercest passions, whether of advocacy or condemnation. His theatrical beginnings with Portable Theatre — one of the itinerant, small-scale groups so redolent of the spirit of 1968 — were very much of their times, and he has remained deeply loyal to the political instincts of that period: yet he has also felt the need for the resources of large stages, and has been no less loyal as almost 'poet-in-ordinary' to the increasingly 'establishment'-oriented National Theatre. Few writers of his stature have worked so frequently in collaboration (still fewer so successfully), yet his voice is also entirely distinctive in that 'strangeness' through which, as Harold Hobson once put it, 'ever so slightly the bones are ill at ease in their sockets'.

The bitter controversy over his most notorious play, *The Romans in Britain*, is here given its due share of attention, for not only does it reflect, from several points of view, vitally important social and dramaturgical issues, but it also stakes out Brenton's territory as a highly *public* playwright. Few but he could have written (with David Hare) what has proved to be his most 'popular' play, *Pravda*, on the seemingly arid theme of press monopoly, and in one way it is perhaps unrepresentative of his work — yet if its spirit is uncharacteristically joyful in its derision, its vision of late-capitalist society is no less ultimately sombre than that of *The Churchill Play* or *Weapons of Happiness*. Televiewers who found themselves baffled and infuriated by his meta-thriller, *Dead Head*, nonetheless tended to remain rivetted to the end: and it is notable that even his most scathing critics can seldom muster their ultimate put-down of boredom against him. Brenton's plays always *provoke* — whether to rage, or to the shocked recognition of shared values suddenly seen in new perspectives — and the present collection helpfully reminds us not only of the variety of responses to his work, but also of the variety of the work itself.

Simon Trussler

1942 13 December, born in Portsmouth, Hampshire. 'I was a "Blitz baby". I was in an Anderson shelter within a few hours, my mother tells me.' ('Petrol Bombs through the Proscenium Arch', p. 5.) Father a policeman who later became a Methodist minister. 'I was brought up in this tiny council house . . . in Bognor with policemen's families' ('Ronald Hayman talks to Howard Brenton', p. 57).

1951 Writes his first play, based on Harris Tweed in the *Eagle* comic.

1953 Grammar school in Chichester, Sussex. 'I was a state school kid. It was a very vicious school. I'm glad now that the grammar schools are going. I think they are as harmful, socially, as public schools' ('Petrol Bombs', p. 5).

1960 Wrote a life of Hitler which he subsequently destroyed. Moved to Castleford, Yorkshire, and taught in local secondary schools. Later moved to Ebbw Vale, Wales. 'In the Methodist Church, if you join late, you get all the hard churches' ('Ronald Hayman talks to Howard Brenton', p. 57).

1962 Went to St. Catherine's College, Cambridge, after deciding against studying painting. 'I soon gave up lectures and wrote all the time, and acted and ran a magazine — an appalling rag — for a while' ('Petrol Bombs', p. 5). Also wrote poems and three novels, 'which taught me to type'.

1965 His first play, *Ladder of Fools*, 'a huge, jokeless, joyless allegory', performed at Cambridge. Obtained a B.A. in English Literature.

1966-68 Worked in various jobs, including the civil service, and as a stage manager and bit-part actor in provincial reps. *It's My Criminal* given a Sunday night 'production without decor' at the Royal Court Theatre in 1966. A shortened, rewritten version of *Ladder of Fools*, *Winter Daddykins*, performed in November of the same year by a touring company directed by Chris Parr. Also wrote an unperformed three act play, *The Plague Garden*, a modern Decameron with a demonic German protagonist. Joined the Brighton Combination as an actor and writer. Wrote *Gargantua* and *A Sky Blue Life*, which were directed by Chris Parr.

1969 *Gum and Goo* performed by Brighton Combination in London, and later at Bradford University with *Heads* and *The Education of Skinny Spew*. Met David Hare at one of Portable

Theatre's first productions, Kafka's *Amerika* at the Arts Lab, where he was the only person in the audience. Hare commissioned *Christie in Love*. *Revenge* performed at the Royal Court Theatre Upstairs. Awarded Arts Council Bursary for 1969-70, and joint winner of the John Whiting award for *Christie in Love*.

1970   Married Jane Fry, a translator. 'I was a fearfully sexist playwright before I met Jane, the women in my plays were lovely but fearsome creatures' ('Playwright for Today', p. 18). They have two sons, born in 1975 and 1977. *Fruit*, a satirical lampoon for the General Election, performed by Portable Theatre.

1971   *Lay By*, the first collaborative work by seven Portable Theatre writers, performed at the Edinburgh Festival and in London.

1972   *Hitler Dances*, a group-devised collaboration with the Traverse Workshop, performed in Edinburgh, directed by Max Stafford-Clark. *Measure for Measure*, a modern burlesque version of Shakespeare satirizing Enoch Powell, performed at the Northcott Theatre, Exeter, directed by William Gaskill, amid much controversy. *England's Ireland*, the second Portable group collaboration, opened at the Mickery, Amsterdam, after more than 50 theatres in Britain turned it down. Portable Theatre disbanded. Brenton appointed resident playwright at the Royal Court Theatre for 1972-73. His film script, *Skinflicker* (originally a TV play but rejected by the BBC), produced by the British Film Institute and directed by Tony Bicât, and his first television play, *Lushly*, transmitted on BBC TV. Also wrote an unproduced TV play, *Our Deep Cold*, 'a filthy piece of sexual liberation', which provided the inspiration for the later play *Sore Throats*.

1973   *Magnificence* performed at the Royal Court in its downstairs auditorium. Collaborated with David Hare on *Brassneck*, a comedy about corruption in the Midlands, for the Nottingham Playhouse. Adapted Genet's *The Screens* for the Bristol New Vic.

1974   *The Churchill Play* performed at the Nottingham Playhouse. Commissioned to write a new play for the National Theatre by Peter Hall. *Rampage*, a film script, commissioned but not produced by United Artists.

1975   *A Saliva Milkshake* transmitted on BBC TV, later performed in a stage version at the Soho Poly. *Government Property*, a reworking of themes from *The Churchill Play* and *Rampage*, produced in Aarhus, Denmark, by Jane Howell. *Jedefrau*, a feminist version of *Everyman*, reproduced by Robert Walker at the Saltzburg Mozart Festival. *Brassneck* transmitted on BBC TV.

1976 *Weapons of Happiness*, directed by David Hare at the National Theatre, wins the *Evening Standard* Best Play Award. *The Paradise Run* transmitted by Thames TV, directed by Michael Apted. Brenton an active member of the London-based Theatre Writers' Union.

1977 *Epsom Downs* commissioned and performed by Joint Stock at the Roundhouse Theatre, London, directed by Max Stafford-Clark.

1978 *A Saliva Milkshake* performed at the Theatre at St. Clements, New York. *Deeds* written in collaboration with Trevor Griffiths, David Hare and Ken Campbell as a farewell for Richard Eyre at the Nottingham Playhouse.

1979 A revised version of *The Churchill Play* performed by the Royal Shakespeare Company at the Warehouse. *Sore Throats* performed by the Royal Shakespeare Company at the Warehouse, directed by Barry Kyle.

1980 *A Short Sharp Shock!*, a satire on the Thatcher government written with Tony Howard, presented at the Theatre Royal, Stratford East, directed by Robert Walker. The Minister for the Arts, Norman St. John Stevas, who did not see the play, apologised to the House of Commons for the show's presentation in a subsidized theatre after complaints were made about the Greater London Council's financial support for the play. Brenton's translation of Brecht's *Life of Galileo* produced at the National Theatre. *The Romans in Britain* also performed at the National Theatre. Mary Whitehouse, who did not see the play, sued its director, Peter Bogdanovich, under the Sexual Offences Act of 1956, for 'procuring an act of gross indecency' after hearing about a scene in the play in which a Druid is raped by a Roman soldier. The prosecution's case was eventually withdrawn on a *nolle prosequi* in 1982, after a great deal of debate about the play and the court case had taken place in the media.

1981 *Thirteenth Night* performed by the Royal Shakespeare Company at the Warehouse, directed by Barry Kyle.

1982 Brenton's new version of Büchner's *Danton's Death*, based on a translation by Jane Fry, performed at the National Theatre. Invited to visit war-torn Beirut by the Bertrand Russell Peace Foundation.

1983 *Sleeping Policemen*, written with Tunde Ikoli, performed in a touring production by Foco Novo, for whom Brenton also adapted Brecht's *Conversations in Exile*. *The Genius* performed at the Royal Court Theatre. *Thirteenth Night* transmitted on BBC Radio.

1984 *The Genius* performed at the Mark Taper Forum, Los Angeles. Invited to the Australian National Playwrights' Conference as guest writer. *Bloody Poetry* performed by Foco Novo. *Desert of Lies* transmitted on BBC TV. *Thirteenth Night* performed by the Brecht Company, Ann Arbor, Michigan.

1985 *Pravda*, written in collaboration with David Hare, presented at the National Theatre, directed by Hare with Anthony Hopkins as the protagonist, Lambert Le Roux. *Pravda* ran for more than a year, and won seven awards, including *Plays and Players* and *Evening Standard* Best Play. Invited to Frascati, Italy, as UK representative at an International Theatre Conference. Completed a TV pilot script, *The Crusaders*.

1986 Four-part TV thriller series, *Dead Head*, transmitted on BBC TV, reached the top ten in the audience ratings. Invited to Germany on a lecture tour of universities. Productions of *Pravda* opened in Christchurch, Adelaide, Hamburg, Brussels, and Tokyo. *Bloody Poetry* produced Off-Broadway. Completing a film script, *The Eleventh Crushing*, part of which is set in Australia, and a Utopian play, *All Tomorrow's Parties*.

a: Apprentice Plays

Ladder of Fools

Play in two acts.
First production: Cambridge University, 1965. Regarded by
   author as apprentice work.
Unpublished.

---

*A violent, allegorical, operatic dream play about a holy
fool living in a tyrannical, subterranean science fiction
world, and his attempt to break out of it. An intruder
into this world dies half-way through the play, and then
proceeds to repeat his part backwards.*

The play was unworkable — the language was so ornate.
There was a lot about dying animals in *Ladder of Fools* — and
there was one twenty minute speech. Every thirty seconds
during that speech someone used to leave the theatre. I left
Cambridge in a drunken neurotic state. It took a long time to
get over being taught literature in that way. And my effort to
write a long play with a great deal of seriousness had burnt me
badly.

Brenton, quoted by Peter Ansorge,
'Underground Explorations No. 1', p. 14

It's My Criminal

First production: Royal Court Theatre, London,
   21 August 1966 (dir. Ian Watt–Smith). Considered by the
   author as apprentice work.
Unpublished.

---

*A two-hander set on an allotment, where a thief is
sleeping rough in an old man's shed, and makes a
farcical, unwitting attempt to burgle the house of a
retired master criminal, whose sidekick punishes him.*

Winter

First production: in a triple bill at the Nottingham Playhouse,
    27 November 1966 (dir. Chris Parr). Considered by author as
    apprentice work.
Unpublished.

A reworked version of Ladder of Fools, *originally written in
verse, but developed into a farce in condensed prose. A father is
dying, and a likely lad pursues his daughter, but is ensnared by
the family.*

---

b: Stage Plays

Gum and Goo

A short one act play.
First production: by the Brighton Combination, January 1969
    (dir. Ruth Marks). Subsequently performed many times throughout
    1969 and 1970 by the Bradford University Theatre Group (dir.
    Chris Parr, with Michele Ryan, Greg Philo, and Phil Emmanuel).
    Revived: Royal Shakespeare Company at the Open Space Theatre,
    London, 22 Feb. 1971 (dir. Janet Henfrey).
Published: in *Plays for Public Places* (Methuen, 1972) and *Plays for
    the Poor Theatre* (Methuen, 1980).

---

*Two boys come across an autistic girl while they are playing.
They are taken aback by her lurid fantasies, particularly her
desire to play a Dracula game. She transforms them into Gum
and Goo, two fantasy gremlins. She then meets a Dirty Old Man
with whom she is about to go off when she is intercepted by a
policeman. Finally the two boys push her down a hole, and she
is found there by a police search party, 'not dead — worse, she's
silent'.*

Gum and Goo was written at the Brighton Combination in January of
1969. A Teachers Conference asked for a show. There were eight days to

do something. We kicked ideas around for two days from a scene I'd
written about a little girl down a hole. I wrote the script in the next two
days. The remaining four days we rehearsed it . . . so the play was
'tailor–made'. A response to an invitation to perform, with what was to
hand — three actors, a few days, a budget of thirty shillings for a ball
and three bicycle lamps.

Brenton, 'Author's Note', *Plays for the Poor Theatre*, p. 56

Howard Brenton is often described as a dramatist who has dragged the
comic strip into the theatre. His archetypal characters certainly revel in
terse sloganizing, but his gift is that of a satirist with ears and eyes
beneath dirty underwear and inside heads where dark phantasies
accumulate. His plays are short and careful structures, showing a flair for
visual theatre, trailing memorably into surrealism and using a language
which owes something to Orton. . . .

Nicholas de Jongh, *'Gum and Goo'*, *The Guardian*, 23 Feb. 1971

Part of Brenton's appeal is that he has jettisoned all the standard devices
of dramatic narrative and reinvented theatre from the nursery level. His
plays generally have a large number of characters and very small casts.
Anybody can be anybody else, or anything else; and as soon as a
dramatic point has been made the action can at once move on elsewhere.

He holds audiences by showing them games which everyone has
played in childhood, and developed them to a point of skill and deadly
intention which children have no time to develop for themselves. . . .
Brenton's trick is to take the murderous and corrupted fantasies of
children, which amuse adults so much, and treat them as real..

Irving Wardle, 'A Game Called Arthur', *The Times*, 24 Feb. 1971

Heads

First production: by the University of Bradford Drama Group,
June 1969 (dir. Chris Parr). *Revived:* by Inter Action at the Ambiance-
in-Exile Lunch Hour Theatre Club, 2 March 1970 (dir. Roland Rees).
Published: in *Christie in Love and Other Plays* (Methuen, 1970) and in
Plays for the Poor Theatre.

*Megan is in love with two men — Brian, an intellectual
weakling, and Rock, a dim-witted muscle-man. She resolves her*

dilemma by chopping off both men's heads and sticking Brian's head on Rock's body, and vice versa. Rock's head and Brian's body go off together and live in a cave, where they are later joined by their 'better halves', who have fled from Megan. The two composite people gradually evolve from their stereotypes into more human creatures, who decide to live as hermits and look after each other's needs.

Heads is a diagrammatic but oddly touching little fable. A girl torn between love for two men, one for his mind, the other for his physique, forces them to switch heads. Instead of marrying her, the resulting superman goes off with the resulting feeble moron: brain and strength, refusing to deny their kinship with weakness. It could be an image of Brenton's own talent and purpose. Both deserve watching.

Ronald Bryden, 'A Criminal Talent', *The Observer*, 15 March 1970

Two neat, slight *faux-naif* sketches . . . make, with jocular brutality, his customary points about the way people get type-cast by life. Brenton's technique recalls the hard-edged outline and brittle dialogue of strip cartoons.

D.A.N. Jones, 'Black Irish', *The Listener*, 12 March 1970

The Education of Skinny Spew

First production: in double bill with *Heads*, June 1969.
Published: in *Christie in Love and Other Plays*, and *Plays for the Poor Theatre.*

While still in the womb, Skinny Spew addresses the audience with the wit and wisdom of an adult. After his birth, he is disgusted at the way his parents treat him like a moron, and drowns them. He is put in an orphanage, but escapes, is given a lift by a pederast, and finally captured by the police. After being subjected to the rigid strictures of a solid education, he reverts to babyhood.

Now in several of the new underground groups one finds a fascination with childhood — a return to the games one played as children. Education, present day adult society, are usually portrayed as corrupt,

14

calcifying influences on younger, more creative energies. Brenton's *The Education of Skinny Spew* is a typical work in this respect as it suggests that growing up under present day conditions is an inherently damaging experience. So, on the one hand, playing games, returning to childhood, can be viewed as a creative act. Indeed those activities can be interpreted as a metaphor of the theatre itself which J. Huizinga points out in his classic study of games theory entitled *Homo Ludens* (Man at Play).

Peter Ansorge, Disrupting the Spectacle, p. 7-8

Most of Brenton's early plays were concerned with children. In them he presented a simplified, scaled-down world in which the children are not portrayed as embryonically radical creatures in an innocent world, but as disturbingly frank examples of the aggressive animality that surrounds them in the grown-up society. Their playgrounds are urban battlefields of blood and sex, and their behaviour denies the premises of all liberal educational theory. . . .

The vision of society presented is bleak, but these early plays do not depend on any depth of characterization or profundity of insight for their success. Everything is stripped down to bare essentials, whilst still leaving the protagonists with an almost poetically released rhetoric in which to articulate their thoughts. . . .

John Bull, New British Political Dramatists, p. 30-2

Revenge

A two act play.
First production: at the Royal Court Theatre Upstairs,
   2 September 1969 (dir. Chris Parr, with John Normington as Hepple and MacLeish).
Published: Methuen, 1970 and 1982.

Adam Hepple, a petty criminal with delusions of grandeur, has become an anachronism in the rapidly advancing world of crime. He is released from Brixton gaol and sets about avenging himself on MacLeish, the Scotland Yard police commissioner who has continually dogged his career. He succeeds only in killing P. C. Albert, an educated, new-style policeman whose ghost appears to Hepple in Brixton and opens the prison gate for him. Albert then warns MacLeish that Hepple is out for

*vengeance. Hepple is about to kill MacLeish with an axe when
both discover they have dreamed this final encounter, and die
the following day, in the 1980s, which have realized Hepple's
hopes and MacLeish's fears of a totally criminalized England.*

It took three years to write, and was in a huge form at first, about five
hours long. Politically I had no ideas, I was very immature. But I had an
instinct that there was a conflict I wanted to get at, between public
figures . . . like a criminal, an old lag from the East End of London, and
a religious, almost ancestral, policeman from Scotland. . . .

It had very literary beginnings in that it was going to be a rewrite of
King Lear, no less, and there still are the *Lear* elements there, in that the
criminal has two daughters and he gives up his kingdom and tries to get
it back and fails. And they never mention the mother, which is one of the
oddly crucial things about *Lear*: Mrs. Lear is never present. . . . Jokes are
really the sinews of that play.

Brenton, in 'Petrol Bombs', p. 8

Rather in the Peter Barnes manner, Brenton's style is on the surface a bit
slapstick, while underneath there dwells a seriousness of intent which
still never loses touch with the inherent theatricality of the writing. The
dual heroes of his sparkling modern melodrama are Adam Hepple, a
faded small-time criminal determined to emulate Capone, and
MacLeish, Scottish hell-fire Assistant Commissioner of Police, whose
mission is to rid the world of such evils before his inevitable retirement
to Paradise.

Frank Cox, 'Revenge', *Plays and Players*, Oct. 1969, p. 40

The murder of Albert is presented in a very stylized way. The scene, in
fact, might be based on the film which first presented audiences with PC
George Dixon — now of TV's Dock Green — entitled *The Blue Lamp*.
. . . As in *Revenge* a melodramatic outrage is expressed by London's
policemen at the murder of one of their kind. Brenton is again revealing
how many of our ideas about crime, law and order stem, in fact, from
sheer fantasy in the form of hackneyed 'cops and robbers' movies.

Peter Ansorge, *Disrupting the Spectacle*, p. 5-6

Christie in Love

A play in eleven scenes.

First production: by Portable Theatre at the Oval House, London, 23
Nov. 1969 (dir. David Hare, with William Hoyland as Christie).
Published: in *Christie in Love and Other Plays* and *Plays for the
Poor Theatre*.

*A Constable and an Inspector exchange dirty jokes as they dig
in a pen of old newspapers, which represent the garden of the
famous criminal John Christie, looking for the corpses of his
victims. Christie rises, Dracula-style, from under the newspapers, and the Inspector interrogates him about his sexual
assaults. The Constable uses a large doll to goad Christie into a
re-enactment of one of his crimes. The two policemen, enraged
by the fact that Christie is such a shy, ordinary person, and not
the diabolical maniac they imagined, hang him in a frenzy of
accusations, and bury him under the newspapers.*

Like Brenton's full-length play *Revenge*, it uses the crude, direct
stylizations of melodrama to remind you that famous crimes have
always been a staple of the popular theatre, whose artificiality distances
their horror. But it gives them an ulterior purpose. By exaggerating
parodically melodrama's back-and-white morality, it underlines how
arbitrary morals are: how little divides criminal from victim or pursuer.
. . . I suspect that in Brenton we may have the British theatre's first
major disciple of Genet — consciously or unconsciously, the ending
of *Revenge*, with villains and police taking their places in the same
bloodstained Valhalla, echoes that of Genet's *Screens*. Like Genet, he
feels for the outcast . . .

He uses mime and ritual in the Genet manner, and has a similar
gift for a mock-heroic rhetoric of thieves' kitchen, prison-cell and
charge-room. But he's less sentimentally involved with his criminals,
clearer about his ultimate strategy to show the unreality of straight
lines in a curved universe, of the roles society forces on us.

Ronald Bryden, 'A Criminal Talent', *The Observer*, 15 March 1970

Christie's first appearance is in the Dracula tradition. Happy horror,
creeps and treats. He rises from the grave luridly, in a frightening
mask. It looks as if a juicy evening's underway, all laughs, nice
shivers, easy oohs and aahs.

But that's smashed up. The lights are slammed on, and the mask is
seen as only a tatty bit of papier mâché. Off it comes, and what's left
is a feeble, ordinary man blinking through his pebble glasses. . . .

I'm setting down the devices I tried to use in the show. That's the basic one. A kind of dislocation, tearing one style up for another, so the proceedings lurch and all interpretations are blocked, and the spectator hunting for easy meaning wearies, and is left only with Christie and his act of love.

Brenton, 'Author's Production Note',
Plays for the Poor Theatre, p. 26

The whole intent of the play is to suggest that, from Christie's point of view, love can be precisely this — 'a corpse, in a dirty garden'. The Constable's idea of love, based on romantic notions derived from popular music, is far less convincing in the context of the 'dirty garden' in which he is searching for the victims of a lover. Christie killed, concludes Brenton, whenever he loved. The Inspector reflects this judgment. Society, he says, has 'got to keep love in bounds. Else it gets criminal'. Obviously Brenton regards the theatre as a place in which the surface 'bounds' of social conduct are broken, and where the monsters resting beneath the surface can make a startling reappearance. But in *Christie in Love*, and this in my view is the weakness of the piece, Brenton never offers us his own verdict on the murderer who so fascinates him. Christie is simply part of a sinister natural process — like the sexual disgust expressed in the Constable's nauseous limericks.

Peter Ansorge, *Disrupting the Spectacle*, p. 5

The search for something other than what Brecht was doing goes on endlessly amongst the writers of my generation, and it was in a sense an alienation device, because the surroundings are highly artificial. There was an attempt to look very hard at Christie, almost like a Bacon painting, where you have an absolutely hard edge, definite. Only a painter could invent that world, yet what's inside that world is a writhing live mess, and that's what I wanted for the play. . . . I had the idea that the policeman in Christie would be like a Kodak camera girl outside a chemist's shop, who is flat, a flat photograph, not a living thing. A caricature. And if you can imagine walking by that and brushing against it and suddenly you realize that the hand is real, and it grabs you, and she says 'You touched me!' That's the sort of development I wanted with *Christie in Love*.

Brenton, 'Petrol Bombs . . . ', p. 8

Wesley

A short play in eight scenes.
First production: Eastbrook Hall Methodist Church at the
    Bradford Festival, 27 Feb. 1970 (dir. Chris Parr).
Published: in *Plays for Public Places*.

*Episodes from the life of John Wesley, with sermons, choir and
an announcer. A simple and comic depiction of Wesley's austere
upbringing, his escape from villagers who attempt to burn down
his father's rectory, his unpopularity at Oxford, his unsuccessful
journey to America to convert the Indians, and his 'dark night of
the soul', which is conveyed in a deliberately anti-climactic way,
as an encounter with two devils in black raincoats.*

The play is a giant blow-up of Wesley's account of his faith. 'Ladies and
gentlemen. We give you John Wesley. The dark night of his soul. His
struggle with sin within. His struggle to know God. His journey to
salvation.'

Brenton, 'Author's Note', *Plays for Public Places*

Wesley . . . saw the whole world just as a matter of faith. . . . I wanted to
write . . . not a Christian play, but I did want to capture all that's
dignified in Methodism. I wanted to give it some expression.

Brenton, 'Petrol Bombs . . .', p. 12

. . . A transformation play which takes a serious look at the founder of
the Methodist church and, indeed, premiered in a church. In this rich mix
of Brechtian narration, choir singing, and complex pantomime, *Wesley*
escapes his dark night of the soul by jettisoning fears of his own
sinfulness in favour of a God-given state of grace. Brenton handles
Wesley's Atlantic crossing much as American dramatist Paul Foster
handled Paine's in *Tom Paine* [1967]. The dozen-member cast of
Wesley is called upon to create ship, storm, and crew through
pantomime.

Roger Cornish, 'Howard Brenton', in
British Dramatists Since World War II, p. 103

Fruit

A short two act play.
First production: by Portable Theatre at the Royal Court Theatre
    Upstairs, in a double bill with David Hare's *Whatever Happened to
    Blake*, 28 September 1970 (dir. David Hare).
Unpublished.

'Fruit *is a play of slanders, lies, torture, perversions in high
places, vile plans in low places, a rotting bag of half truths for
an audience to throw where they will,' announce the play's
opening lines. Paul, a thalidomide victim who has become an
osteopath, watches the 1970 General Election on TV,
commenting on the obscenity of the public spectacle. Paul is
visited by the alcoholic Labour ex-Prime Minister, who
confronts him with a blackmail tape which reveals that Paul's
chauffeur is having an affair with the Tory Prime Minister. Paul
attempts to blackmail the Prime Minister, who simply sets the
police on his trail. A newspaper commissions Paul's wife to
write her memoirs, while Paul falls through the bottom of
England, where he meets an ageing Leninist who reprimands
him for his bad historical analysis, and teaches him to make a
petrol bomb, which is thrown into the audience.*

In writing *Fruit* I was influenced by some French situationist texts . . .
The situationists describe our world as 'the society of the spectacle'.
There is a screen called public life which is reported on the telly and in
the newspapers. This version of public life is a spectacle, it operates
within its own laws. It's a vast, intricate confidence game. The last
general election was a tight, fraudulent spectacle. So we've become very
cynical about public life — just as the politicians are totally cynical. In
Fruit a man, for reasons of personal revenge and cynicism, tries to bring
down the government — by blackmailing the prime minister, threatening
to expose the MP's homosexuality. But he finds that the 'spectacle'
caters for this kind of attack. It will have nothing to do with him.

Brenton, quoted by Peter Ansorge, in
'Underground Explorations 1', p. 16

. . . The play ends by pointing out that there could have been another
attack, mounted from another angle, a much more political, realistic one.

20

That, in a sense, is the open-endedness of it.

First, 'Is the Prime Minister a homosexual? Do I care?' A lot of people in the audiences have happened to believe that that line is right. In the discussions after the play, they were often very angry indeed. David Hare staged it deliberately against what is regarded as elegant theatre, which is what the piece needed, dirty linen. It had a scrubbed kind of staging which wasn't pleasing to the eye, only pleasing to a sense of the play, and in a way was very beautiful, so functional. It was just after the General Election, so all the questions were about 'Is that true?' It went to Holland and English theatre there, even when it's true, turns immediately into 'art'. . . . The Dutch critics and audiences had seen this as a rewrite of *Richard III*, but [an] Englishman realized what it was, a blatant, black attack.

Brenton, quoted by Jonathan Hammond, 'Messages First', p. 26-7

Brenton's 'satire on the future' is actually a wildly caricatured *Private Eye* fantasia on a fairly recognizable political present, in which politicians of both parties merge in one bland conspiracy to maintain power and appearances. . . . Brenton never really finds a way to end the piece, or give it a point, but he shows here and there the same vein of sardonic *News of the World* poetry which distinguished *Christie in Love*.

Ronald Bryden, 'Back to old Symbolia', *The Observer*, 4 Oct. 1970

Where the play fails for me is in the nihilism at its core. The telly satirists in the mid-60s had purpose behind their lampoonings. Brenton bowls over his iron-fisted nancy-boy Prime Minister with the same evident relish that he puts the boot into his masochistic Welsh former Cabinet minister, but to no apparent end. One cannot really believe that the state of British parliamentary democracy, and our society in general, is as sick as its author would have us believe.

'Edinburgh Fringe', *Sunday Telegraph*, 6 Sept. 1970

Scott of the Antarctic
  or, What God Didn't See

A play in nineteen scenes.
First production: Mecca Ice Rink for the Bradford Festival, 1971
  (dir. Chris Parr).
Published: in *Plays for Public Places*.

A mock 'spectacle on ice', caricaturing the notions of heroism in the Polar expeditions. King George V throws a tantrum when he discovers the South Pole is not part of the British Empire, and complains to God, who sends him the English hero Scott. The Devil appears on a motorbike in company with a hell's angel to thwart the expedition, and presents the madness of Evans and the death of Oates as cabaret turns.

I'm very interested in people who could be called saints, perverse saints, who try to drive a straight line through very complex situations, and usually become honed down to the point of death. Scott was one of those. Scott's expedition failed because it was planned, all those stores, all the teams and procedures, were planned for four people. . . .

Scott was not on the ice to get to the pole. He couldn't skate in fact — he kept tumbling over. He was there because of his public school, his C. of E. religion and the British Empire. . . . The project was ripe for breakdown.

Brenton, in 'Underground Explorations 1', p. 16

A Sky Blue Life

Scenes after Maxim Gorky.
First production: Little Theatre, St. Martin's Lane, 1966 (dir. Chris Parr)
    Revised version at the Open Space Theatre, London, 18 Nov. 1971
    (dir. Walter Donohue), and at Bristol New Vic, 31 Oct. 1972.
Unpublished.

Seven sparse and continuous scenes present vignettes from the life of Gorky, exploring his conflicts with Lenin's revolutionary programme. Gorky takes part in scenes from his work, including Ice, *about walking on the frozen water of the Volga, and* The Depths, *a version of* The Lower Depths, *in which he struggles against the play's sentimental momentum. He meets Tolstoy, a senile and demented symbol of the old Russia, and Lenin, who breaks up* The Depths, *denounces it as 'bourgeois crap', and urges Gorky to write pamphlets instead. In* The Dead Man, *a family of pig farmers persuade Gorky to perform the father's last rites with a pig farming manual instead of a bible, and in* A Birthday *he is forced to act as a midwife, watched by Lenin.*

Brenton's terse, economical style (shared with Snoo Wilson and other Portable Theatre-reared writers) was peculiarly effective in illuminating Gorky's talent through carefully chosen scenes from his life and through showing him in relation to his source material. . . . The whole play was, incidentally, an excellent introduction to the works and talent of Gorky for the uninitiated.

> Jonathan Hammond, 'Lunch-Time Line-Up', *Plays and Players*,
> Jan. 1972, p. 51

Hitler Dances

Play in twenty-four scenes, written in collaboration with the
    Traverse Workshop.
First production: Traverse Theatre, Edinburgh, 20 January 1972
    (dir. Max Stafford-Clark), and subsequently at the Royal Court
    Theatre Upstairs, June 1972.
Published: Methuen, 1982.

A long and freewheeling play written collectively from individual responses to the Second World War, debunking the way it has been mythologized in fiction, films, and television. The company call up Hans, a dead German soldier, whose puppet-like actions provide a focal point for children's games. The story of the British special agent Violette Szabo, as portrayed in the film Carve Her Name with Pride, *is presented with an anti-romantic slant, with the cast goading one another into expressions of violence.*

Hitler Dances shares many themes and techniques with those early plays, *Gum and Goo*, *Heads*, and *The Education of Skinny Spew* (all 1969). What was different in the case of *Hitler Dances*, however, was that with the Traverse company, Brenton was using a group that had been committed for some time to exploring and developing new relationships between writers and actors in the production of a play. . . . It is perhaps the least conventional of all Brenton's plays. It is certainly the least accessible on a first reading. Its structure appears to be disjointed and fragmented: the two stories that are told constantly overlap and undercut each other, violently impacting together the people, places and historical situations that are separated in reality by many years and miles. Moreover, the play refuses to be pinned down into a

23

single recognizable theatrical genre. Styles change with bewildering speed from gothic melodrama to breezy naturalism to two-dimensional satire; powerful images spring up, only to be savagely cut down by a sudden, deflating joke.

Richard Boon, 'Introduction', *Hitler Dances*, p. vii

What *do* we mean when we describe Hitler as 'a monster'? The actors in *Hitler Dances* had to move between fact and fiction, the truth about the war and the myths. By changing from monsters into men, from heroines into social victims, from Dam Busting heroes to timid boozers terrified by the prospect of fighting, *Hitler Dances* produced a style of performance which mirrored a contrast between fact and fiction, truth and lies. . . .

Peter Ansorge, *Disrupting the Spectacle*, p. 51

How Beautiful with Badges

A short play in six scenes.
First production: Open Space Theatre, London, 2 May 1972
   (dir. Walter Donohue).
Unpublished.

Tony, a tortured young working class Maoist disguised as a boy scout, and his timid and childish sidekick Ian become involved in a confrontation with two hell's angels, Gut the Buzzard and Child Molester, who are on an acid trip. Tony is beaten almost to death with chains. Christ appears, and unsuccessfully tries to nail himself up on to the cross.

Plays are not critical in the way that an essay, a speech, or an argument are. There's no real dialectic in a play, only one view. Everything in the play is rigged — the dialectic exists between the play and the audience. . . . Tony is a totally fucked-up character, the way he's fucked up is quite pitiful, ludicrous and comic; he's a clown, and the points he makes are not to be analyzed like a careful drawing. Maoism and British uniform fascism have a life of their own. Tony stirs it up, and just peels the orange in that particular way, and if anyone sees the light that's fine. . . . *Badges* was written as a response to the Bob Dylan song 'All Along the Watchtower' which I still find incomprehensible. The two riders are the hell's angels in the play, and there's the joker and the thief. It's an unargued play.

Brenton, in an unpublished interview with Tony Mitchell, 1974

How Beautiful with Badges shows, with the author's customary sharpness and precision, how a young man fucked up by his bourgeois, right-wing background hangs on to his Maoist political beliefs as a lifeline to maintain some kind of balance and sanity.

Jonathan Hammond, *Contemporary Dramatists*, p. 118

Measure for Measure

A comedy in two acts, adapted from Shakespeare.
First production: Northcott Theatre, Exeter, 25 Sept. 1972
   (dir. William Gaskill).
Unpublished.

A Macmillan-like Duke hands over his power to a Powell-like Angelo, who immediately gets an anti-pornography campaign under way. Isabella is the Salvation Army sister of a black pop artist and porn film star, Claudio, whose director, Jerky Joe, becomes concerned when his hot property is jailed. The Duke disguises himself as a member of the Salvation Army and gets Jerky Joe to film Angelo's seduction of Isabella's stand-in. Angelo, helped by the prison governor, gets Claudio executed, and the Duke is put out to graze and write his memoirs. Angelo continues to rule, illustrating that the 'old order, unchecked, will bring about a new and harsher form of itself'.

I knew Exeter was a High Tory town and that, if you're going to have stage time there and you're trying to write a comedy, then it had to be funny. And it had to go. And it had to be clear. And you had to drive it very, very hard, because they wouldn't give an inch. And why should they, really? The play attacked Powellism blatantly, unfairly and almost as hard as it could go in the middle of what proved to be a very popular show, because it did work as a popular entertainment. . . . It taught me something, that your enemies know what you're doing, they're not bumbling old fools. They [the board of the Northcott Theatre] never once attacked on an artistic front, which we could have fought. It was always the small print of the licensing laws, the refinements of libel . . .

It was the first big theatre that I'd ever written for. I felt I put my head in the door and they had it off by the neck, without any trouble, and that was a terrible lesson.

Brenton, quoted by Jonathan Hammond, 'Messages First', p. 28

Measure for Measure has always been a problem play, difficult to make convincing on the stage whichever scholarly interpretation you apply. With a skill that confirms his reputation as one of the best young dramatists to emerge from the not-so-quiet revolution in the theatre of the past four years, Howard Brenton has turned it, problems and all, into a chillingly persuasive condemnation of the puritan backlash which makes Lord Longford and the Vice Squad the heroes of the hour . . . this Northcott production reminds us that the idealist determined to stamp out corruption is the ally of repression and hypocrisy more vicious by far than the shabby, mildly pathetic commerce in delight of a permissive society. . . . Adapting the classics can be dangerous – like an ill-matched marriage it's apt to make both partners look ridiculous instead of highlighting their virtues — but Howard Brenton has been intelligent as well as audacious in his revisions. The verse has been pared down while the high points are preserved with all their all emotional power; much of the low comedy has been effectively rewritten in a modern idiom . . . The full house on the first night may have come to see Shakespeare, but it was Howard Brenton they were applauding at the end.

Michael Anderson, 'Exeter', *Plays and Players*, Nov. 1972, p. 65-7

Mug

A short one act play.
First production: Inter-Cities Conference, 'More Power to the People', Manchester, 9 June 1973.

An Old Man is fishing on Clapham Common when he is accosted by a Mugger. He squirts CS gas into the Mugger's eyes, and suggests that he learn who his real enemies are. At the end of the play he catches a baby's rattle on his fishing line. A condemnation of 'arty little theatre-plays about violent times' which explores the contradictions between sociological studies of violence and its steady increase.

Magnificence

Play in eight scenes.
First production: Royal Court Theatre, 28 June 1973
    (dir. Max Stafford-Clark, with Kenneth Cranham as Jed).
Published: Methuen, 1973 and 1980.

Five young people squat in an empty London slum house as a
symbolic protest against capitalism and the housing shortage.
After the owner of the house bursts in with the police, Mary, a
pregnant art student, is kicked in the stomach and loses her
baby. Jed, another of the group, is sentenced to nine months in
prison. Alice, a Conservative M.P. in the Ministry for the
Environment, visits Babs, a Macmillan-like former colleague,
who stages his death scene on the Cam. Jed gets out of prison
committed to armed revolutionary struggle, and attempts to
assassinate Alice. The gelignite collar he forces on Alice fails to
explode, and Alice reveals that he has been demoted to Pay-
master General. While the two are talking, the gelignite
explodes and both are killed.

One of my blazing failures as a writer when it comes to agit-prop is that
I understand the 'agit' bit but I have difficulty with the 'prop'. That's
been one of the difficulties with *Magnificence*. I was all raring to go
with the 'agit' — in the sense of stirring things up — but the thought
took time to rein in, hammer down. I set out to write a play which was
more aggressive than *Skinflicker*, a play about a group of people who
really went for the world. As I proceeded I began to realize that this was
impossible. Jed's attitude leads to acts of terrorism which are futile. So
what began to emerge was a kind of tragedy, a tragedy not of pride or of
fate but of waste. There should be a strong sense of waste amongst the
characters — a waste of effort and of thought.
                    Brenton, 'Disrupting the Spectacle', *Plays and Players*,
                                                    July 1973, p. 22-3

I did realize it too late and the structure of the play is badly marred
because of it, but the person who's carrying the wisdom of the play is the
boy Cliff. His knowledge of what's going on and what to do about it and
his sense of the tragedy involved is very strong, but he disappears from
the play. He doesn't occupy a central scene. The central scene is between

the bomber and the guy whose libertarian ideals have decayed. There were ideas in the play which were just not getting a voice and in fact these were the ideas I believed in. So I wrote an epilogue. I had this man come forward and say exactly what I felt about it. It's a very puny ending. You've spent 20 complex minutes staging a dialectical scene where you show the inevitable consequence of that kind of action, which is Beirut — undisciplined, anarchic bombing versus a collapsing middle class. The streets run with blood and politically there's no one to pick up the pieces. That was the political feeling behind the play.

Brenton, interviewed by Ronald Hayman, p. 57

Perhaps Brenton is reacting against the kind of 'radical' drama that turns every representative of the status quo into wind, wool and straw, a caricature so obviously ludicrous that it is a waste of breath to condemn him. If so, he has overcompensated. Those on (broadly) the Right emerge far more strongly from *Magnificence* than those on the Left: it is they who are the more rounded and get the better lines. There's less of that quirky verbal energy which distinguishes Brenton, less imagination and creative zest, in the scenes involving his five embryo revolutionaries than in the episode in which a bailiff and a policeman mooch outside a house in which they're squatting . . .

Benedict Nightingale, 'Jed-Propelled', *New Statesman*, 6 July 1973

The play's dialectic unfortunately does not take place between it and the audience, but between the remains of the author's own liberalism and his emergence into Marxism. Brenton has been criticized by Irving Wardle and Robert Brustein among others for his 'Messages First' doctrine, which has been dubbed by some the 'new brutalism'. It is not a criticism in which I would share. I believe that Brenton is right to emphasize the importance of the message in the present situation, and ignore the Trotskyist and liberal heresies that art and politics only incidentally mix. But the corollary to his approach to playwriting is a very clear-cut explicit political position, which as yet he does not possess. In the last analysis, the play lacks the size and weight, both thematically and formally, to use what Brenton has called the 'moral force' of the Royal Court proscenium to its best effect. Having said that, however, I am equally certain that Brenton has the imagination, intelligence and potential to remedy these defects next time out.

Jonathan Hammond, '*Magnificence*', *Plays and Players*,
Aug. 1973, p. 43

In my view the watershed for the fringe was reached during the run of

Howard Brenton's *Magnificence* in the Royal Court's main auditorium in July. The magnificent point about *Magnificence* was that it created a real talking point among its audiences. Writers, directors and actors who had previously been confined to small-scale shows in tiny environments began to measure the possibilities of working in a large theatre — of reaching wider audiences. The play also contained an interesting message for its audience: it told the familiar story of a group of people who try to set up an alternative way of life in isolation from the rest of society . . .

With hindsight it is tempting to read *Magnificence* as an unconscious critique of the whole fringe movement. The sense of alienation, the attempt to create a different style of life, the increasing reliance on violence, theatrical terrorism, the final sense of political confusion — that mere anger and aggression lead to impotence — these thematic strands seemed to encapsulate the whole dilemma of fringe theatre. Just how ironic in fact was the fact was the title of the play and how 'magnificent' was the rebellion enacted by fringe theatre between 1968 and 1973? A myth or a reality?

Peter Ansorge, 'Green Room', *Plays and Players*, Oct. 1973, p. 19

. . . as a political diagnosis, the piece relies too much on accident. That said, it is scene a wonderful piece of theatre; annexing whole new chunks of modern life and presenting them in a style at once fruitful and magnified; and re-establishing Shaw's point that the more iniquitous a capitalist government, the more charming the people that run it.

Irving Wardle, 'Magnificence', *The Times*, 2 July 1973

The Churchill Play

A four act play, 'as it will be performed in the winter of 1984 by the internees of the Churchill Camp somewhere in England.'
First production: Nottingham Playhouse, 8 May 1974
(dir. Richard Eyre). *Revived:* by the Royal Shakespeare Company at the Warehouse, 11 Apr. 1979 (dir. Barry Kyle).
Published: Eyre Methuen, 1974.

Brenton's contribution to the 1974 Churchill centenary, using Churchill's hereditary syphilis as a symbol of a politically and economically crippled Britain in which the army has assumed a directly political role. The internees of the Churchill Camp, who are all political activists of varying types, prepare to perform a play for a visiting committee from the coalition government, at the behest of the liberal prison doctor, Captain Thompson. They use the performance of the play, a lampoon of Churchill, as a pretext to stage a breakout from the camp, holding the committee members at gunpoint. They are finally forced to give up their escape attempt.

I'd had an idea for a play about Churchill from when I was in the Combination, and I tried to write it first then. But I couldn't make it work. I had the idea of his coming out of the catafalque in Westminister Hall while he was lying in state, coming out and addressing the young soldiers around him. That idea was the beginning, and then there were more recent preoccupations, particularly the truth about Long Kesh. And I wrote a radio play about an internment camp in England in a few years' time. But they wouldn't do it on radio. And I was full of that idea, so I threw the radio play away and re-wrote the whole thing, framing the idea of Churchill in a camp called Churchill, somewhere in England ten years from now. . . . The idea that Churchill is universally admired by people who went through the war is not true, but what they always say, and what my parents say, 'He gave us freedom.' . . . We are in danger of throwing it away — and also . . . it's not freedom. That was the gut feeling behind the play. I also wanted, for the first time, not to write about one single person, but to write about a group of people, who are not particularly intelligent, who are not politically aware, who are not heroic, but together make an almost animal sense. Writing about the prisoners in the camp, that's how I approached them. I didn't want any of them to be saints, just trying to see it through, work it through, and in a sense it became the most dense writing that I've got to — because of that.

Brenton, 'Petrol Bombs . . .', p. 14-15

Like most young British dramatists, Howard Brenton is obsessed with the state of the nation. . . . You come out discussing the truth of the play's ideas rather than its technique; and on this level Brenton is endlessly stimulating. . . . *The Churchill Play* establishes Brenton as a major talent.

Michael Billington, *The Guardian*, 10 May 1974

Mr. Brenton's play amounts to little but a routine disapproval of authority It is talkative but lacks any depth of thought or characterization. . . . To quote Dorothy Parker, there is less in it than meets the eye.

B. A. Young, *Financial Times*, 11 May 1974

Howard Brenton has a terrifying imagination that makes his *The Churchill Play* (Nottingham Playhouse) a very disturbing experience. It is an experience one would not like to have missed, but it unsettles the foundations of the world on which England unsteadily rests. One of the few matters on which it is still generally assumed that there is a consensus of opinion is that in May 1940, England found a man who could, and did, save her. The haunting and alarming suggestion made in Mr. Brenton's powerful play . . . is that the man England found was the wrong man. . . . *The Churchill Play* is a work of great aesthetic and intellectual power, a work as impregnable, self-defended and ambiguous as was Sartre's when Sartre was at the height of his creative power. . . .

Harold Hobson, *The Sunday Times*, 2 June 1974

In *The Churchill Play*, Joby, the interned journalist who plays Churchill in a 1984 internment camp somewhere in England, talks of 'Ten years, the country sliding down. Through the nineteen seventies. Guns. Barbed wire.' All of these [Portable] writers see England in terms of a violent political landscape. But it's at this point that, it seems to me, Brenton has gone further than the others in creating a theatre language in which the violence can be held at arm's length and examined. . . . Brenton goes beyond the formula of instant theatre, instant violence, and instant politics and finds a way of making us look again at the past which has shaped the future into which he sees us drifting. . . .

Brenton's picture of England in the 1970s is as bleak as the wet landscape that surrounds his 1984 internment camp. But what is heartening is the way he uses the rich, theatrical language he and his colleagues have created to confront that bleak situation with intelligence and wit.

Albert Hunt, 'Theatre of Violence', *New Society*, 4 Nov. 1976, p. 262

A roar of motorcycles outside, blinding light from searchlights and the sound of loudspeakers leaves us wondering if any survival is a likely prospect. Brenton's first version ended at this bleak point. His second adds just one line, uttered by a prisoner: 'The Third World War'. The battle between society and its dissidents will continue, intensify, perhaps lead to something new.

Benedict Nightingale, *Fifty Modern British Plays*, p. 446-7

We have been heavily dosed with nightmare plays about Britain's totalitarian future, envisioned as transpiring any time from next decade to next week; this is the daddy of them all — the first, the most ambitious, and considerably the best written. . . . The play [is] a mess . . . It is redeemed . . . by its narrative thrust, and by the power of its dialogue, second only to Edward Bond's; also by the fact that it has a direct line to current fears — witness the number of plays that have cannibalized it since its first prophetic appearance. . . . Mr. Brenton is more forthcoming than most of his successors have been in documenting his nightmare, but like them he can stop short at awkward junctures.

Robert Cushman, 'Mr. Brenton's Original Nightmare',
The Observer, 29 Apr. 1979

Weapons of Happiness

A two act play, commissioned by the National Theatre.
First production: Lyttelton Theatre, 14 July 1976 (dir David Hare,
   with Frank Finlay as Frank, and Julie Covington as Janice).
Published: Eyre Methuen, 1976, and in *Landmarks of Modern British
   Drama: the Plays of the Seventies* (Methuen 1986).

The play is set in . . . a factory, and working in it, like an old tramp, like some old wino, is this fellow they call Joe. He is in fact Josef Frank, who was once a cabinet minister in the first Communist Czech government in the early 1950s. He was caught up in the show trials of 1952, and survived, and is now living in wilful obscurity in London simply because, although he wasn't executed, he feels he has been completely destroyed. And the play is a long resurrection of this man as the young people around him in this factory where he works as a cleaner become angry, realizing what is going on, and decide to try to do something about it. And through a totally unexpected love affair with a young girl who is working in this factory, he becomes involved again. He refuses to do so, and the demands put on him in this London backwater bring up for him the meaning of his life: Stalinism, the European Communist movement, what's happened in Europe, our modern heritage is suddenly in his hands briefly again. And he gives them some simple advice before he dies, before the strain kills him.

Brenton, interviewed by Ronald Hayman, p. 56

I know I'm a bloody-minded, difficult writer; I also happen to know I work best in a theatre, so why not be at the best? David [Hare] and I regard ourselves and our cast and production team as an armoured charabanc full of people parked within the National walls — we've brought our own concept in with us because we want consciously to use the National facilities to show our work off to its best advantage. It's like being given the greatest orchestra in the world to play with. . . . I desperately don't want to be culturally stacked and filed away in some neat slot, and the joy of the theatre is that it's so uncontrolled: if I fail here I can go and work in street theatre . . .

Brenton, quoted by Sheridan Morley,
'The Man Behind the Lyttelton's First New Play',
The Times, 10 July 1976

The poverty of political theatre in England is so great that almost any drama with political intimations gets welcomed as if it were the long-lost grandchild of Bertolt Brecht. It creates a real dilemma for those (like myself) who genuinely hanker for a piece of relevant theatre that isn't ideologically pre-packaged and offensively 'all thought out'. *Weapons of Happiness* is about political subjects but, if your definition of political art includes moral fair-play and aesthetic equilibrium, it is hard to clasp it to one's bosom as a 'political play'. . . .

Brenton is writing out of his convictions. He passionately believes the worker's lot is not a happy one, and that some kind of drastic social upheaval — like a revolution — will redress a lot of the balances. I believe that as well, but I would no sooner attempt merely to posit it as a belief than I would wear a badge proclaiming my love of chocolate milkshakes. My beliefs (and Brenton's) are irrelevant to an artefact that has to accommodate *all* the beliefs engendered by the author's primary conviction. It just isn't enough to edit out disagreeable or unsympathetic ideas because one doesn't agree with them or finds them unsympathetic.

Charles Marowitz, 'Weapons of Happiness',
Plays and Players, September 1976, p. 18-19

What the National gave Brenton above all was the space, the facilities and the size of cast to work properly for the first time on the creation of an 'epic' structure that he had been moving towards in the plays immediately preceding. In *Weapons*, there is no single voice on which the audience can rely. There is a huge, and endlessly shifting, space on which contradiction flourishes. The separate viewpoints are shown to have arisen from the very different *social* experiences of the various protagonists. This multiplicity of viewpoint is central and is reinforced at narrative level by the constant disruption of the 'story', and by the historical jumps. Each scene, in classic Brechtian manner, is in effect a separate discourse with the audience; and the audience is being asked to consider a series of virtual contradictions, which in turn form a larger discourse. No single 'reading' of the play is possible.

John Bull, *New British Political Dramatists*, p. 106

It seems that on occasion Brenton's love of comedy and violent theatrical confrontation robs him of a much-needed analytical element. There is simply very little contest in the play between the capitalist classes and their real or potential opponents, even though the latter comprise a portentous Czech, a deaf mute, an illiterate, an old lag, and a few sullen, inarticulate boys and girls. Nevertheless *Weapons of Happiness* contains much that is good about Brenton's work. It has a dimension that so much political theatre lacks (and not merely because it could utilize the National Theatre's gallery of computerized stage effects), ranging as it does from the New Testament of Christ to the Cosmos of the Planetarium, from the winter streets of post-war Moscow to the rural landscape of contemporary Wales. . . . It is the great achievement of Brenton's play that . . . three assertions are almost simultaneously displayed. Yet the final word is left with the audience.

Steve Grant, 'Voicing the Protest',
Dreams and Deconstructions, p. 120-1

Like Mr. Bond, Mr Brenton deals with revolution, but much more complexly. . . . He has in fact a vision of revolution which is quite extraordinary in its creative ambiguity, its richness, its power to stimulate, to threaten, and to inspire. . . . This is indeed a relevant play.

Harold Hobson, 'Troubled Waters', *Sunday Times,* 18 July 1976

Weapons of Happiness strikes me as profoundly implausible, and also lacking in commodities badly needed when the subject is nothing less than our collective future: intellectual penetration, mental rigour, the will to interpret rather than casually evoke. The National is right to present work which might upset the politically squeamish; but it is not going to achieve much with a play that shares the vagueness, the lack of focus and force, of its potato crisp revolutionaries.

Benedict Nightingale, 'Cheese and Onion',
New Statesman, 23 July 1976

Epsom Downs

A play in two acts, written in collaboration with Joint Stock Theatre
   Company.
First production: by Joint Stock at the Roundhouse, London,
   8 Aug. 1977 (dir Max Stafford-Clark).
Published: Eyre Methuen, 1977.

Written for nine actors who double some fifty parts, including naked men as horses. A kaleidoscopic day at the races in Jubilee year. As the drunken, exposed sex maniac Labour Peer Lord Rack, in a sense the play's chorus, puts it: 'Derby belongs to everyone . . . Only time in their lives ordinary men and women make a decision'. A homeless family quintuple their life savings on Lester Piggot's mount; a stable lad is sacked and picks up a gipsy girl; a trainer and a superintendent oversee the day's proceedings and welcome the Aga Khan and other prestigious horse owners; an Evangelist duo of reformed compulsive gamblers succumb once again to the betting urge. Meanwhile the ghost of Emily Davison, the suffragist who threw herself in front of the King's horse at the 1913 Derby, wanders amidst gipsies, buskers, society denizens, a Kermit frog salesman and a chicken vendor, Jubilee drunks, owners, bookmakers, jockeys and lovers. The race is run and the litter cleared up by inmates from the local asylum.

Joint Stock has a distinctive way of working with a playwright. The final text is the writer's alone, but is written in full view of the company's constant, questioning gaze. I am indebted to them for their painstaking research, their encouragement and stamina, their endless but always creative criticism, their flair and invention in workshops and rehearsals, and for the many happy hours we spent together on race-courses during the flat-racing season of 1977.

Brenton, 'Author's Note', *Epsom Downs*, p. 6

Rarely since the Jacobeans and the classical Japanese theatre have writers collaborated with a company of actors in the way they now work with Joint Stock. . . . theatre on a broad scale which conveys the whole sweep of English society, from the ruling to the workless classes. . . .

Such a loose structure seems, at first, to have no direction, but from the individuals Brenton moulds a crowd. . . .

Into his enthusiasm for his characters, Brenton places a measure of ambivalence. Individuals may win money, but the rich win more. . . . Among the jokes and living characters, Brenton lets Emily Davison's ghost wander, questioning the unthinking homage to the Queen, the lack of protest at social inequalities. It is a flawed dramatic idea, clear enough in its sobering effect, but unsuccessful in deepening the fabric of meaning.

Ned Chaillet, *Plays and Players*, Oct. 1977, p. 22-3

... This piece echoes *Bartholomew Fair*: a great public festival, held on common land and pulling in punters of every degree. ... Half a dozen threads of plot are woven in and out of a teaming Brueghel-like composition. ... Brenton the radical also has his say ... Altogether, a marvel of expressive economy.

> Irving Wardle, *The Times*, 9 Aug. 1977

The play is afflicted by a monotony of rhythm and by the surprisingly low pressure of the writing. This new Derby Day canvas may be Mr. Brenton's most genial play, but it is also his weakest.

> Robert Cushman, 'The Three Irish Maries',
> *The Observer*, 14 Aug. 1977

Howard Brenton's *Epsom Downs* is ... a pastoral belatedly committed to radical politics. It is Frith's *Derby Day* plus marxism plus full-frontals ... Brenton has found here, he believes, 'a metaphor for Britain'. He is not the first to have done so. Frith's painting of the crowd on the Downs ... testifies to the ... Derby as a secular carnival. ...

Brenton's politics are unsound because they're sentimental, but also because they're surreal: his indignation generates a nonsensical extremism which turns cabinet ministers into transvestites (as in *Magnificence*) or, in this case, into scabrous loons, and radicals into mocking cartoonists.

> Peter Conrad, 'Some Versions of "Pastoral" ,'
> *New Statesman*, 12 Aug. 1977

Brenton's portrait of Derby Day, is, like Jonson's play, an exuberant documentary about a secular English festival. ... It doesn't have the old master's ability to make you care about the fate of individual eccentrics, but it gives you a sense of the two nations not quite coming together for a gaudy popular event. ... The result is his most accessible and simply enjoyable play, if not his most astringent.

> Michael Billington, *The Guardian*, 8 Aug. 1977

Sore Throats

'An intimate play in two acts.'
First production: Royal Shakespeare Company at the Warehouse
    Theatre, London, 8 Aug. 1979 (dir. Barry Kyle, with Paola Dionisotti,
    Malcolm Storry, and Ruby Wax.)

Published: in *Sore Throats and Sonnets of Love and Opposition,* (Methuen,1979). Also in *Theater*, XII, No. 2 (Spring 1981).

Judy, a 39-year-old woman, has divorced her policeman husband, Jack, and found a flat on her own, where he confronts her. They abuse each other, and he brutally beats her in his attempts to force her to sign over to him his half of the house, which he has previously told her she can have. He intends to go to Canada with his new girl friend, Celia. Sally, a 23-year-old telephone operator, arrives to look at the flat, which Judy has advertised to share, and drives Jack out. The two women begin a bizarre 'experiment in living', blowing most of Judy's money on sexual experiments, high living, a trip to America, and full-time dedication to sexual gratification. Jack returns to the flat, which has become a total mess, and recounts how he has broken down in a remote part of Canada and had to deliver Celia's baby there. He has since been denied custody of the child, and Celia has left him. He asks Judy for some money. Judy begins tearing up the money she has left, and lights a match, declaring she is 'going to be fucked, happy and free'.

The state-of-the-nation speech in . . . *Sore Throats* . . . has little to do with the rest of the play, which could be going on anywhere . . . The play ends with Judy looking forward to a future of sexual, personal and financial freedom. Mr. Brenton is not usually an ironist so one can only think, bully for you. Other reactions are stifled by the slenderness of his personal documentation. . . . Mr. Brenton's single-mindedness has resulted in emaciation.

> Robert Cushman, 'Going on About England',
> *The Observer*, 2 Sept. 1979

There will certainly be no riot at the Warehouse, with its quotations from Brecht in the programme; its 'Save Our Theatre' leaflets on your seat; its new play by Mr. Brenton, a work of closet misogyny if ever there was one, disguised as Women's Lib (his wife-beating policeman, by whom we are supposed to be shocked, is given all the most sympathetic and personal speeches); and, to delight our eyes, its close-up porn-pic of a black woman's gaping vagina among the litter of the stage set. Theatre workers' acquiescence in such reactionary contradictions can only be due to careerism, apathy, or fear — all stock weapons in the armoury of the power-monolith.

Margaretta D'Arcy, 'Derry Do', New Statesman, 7 Sept. 1979

Didn't Lenin sort
You out bloody years ago?
'Childish disorders'

Fanatical mouths
Stink of a vicious belly
Fermenting hatred

. . .

Filth lies on the stage
You say that makes my play filth —
Censors talk like that

. . .

When peace breaks out
D'Arcy will want a new war
To kill the lovers

D'Arcy can't forgive
Writers for their gentleness
Because she can't write

Writers understand
Hate cannot amplify truth
Contradiction can

You attack my play
Now I attack your review
Who enlightens whom?

Brenton, 'Haiku for Magaretta D'Arcy
on Her Rubbishing of My Play',
New Statesman, 14 Sept. 1979

The material is familiar, and Brenton exploits the familiarity to develop a highly detailed world of 'raging', violence, tenderness and claustrophobia. His accents are harsh. The pressures on his characters are extreme and unremitting. Though there are moments when some glimmer of understanding or some brief moment of personal equilibrium is achieved, these tend to be lost in an everlasting tide of acrimony and frustration. . . . *Sore Throats* is demanding and mostly black theatre which offers little in the way of respite from its commitment to the harsh and often ugly struggle for identity and survival.

Catherine Peake, *Theatre Australia*, April 1980, p. 52

In *Sore Throats* Brenton creates an intricate mesh of money, morals and marriage; he decries a social framework defined by the materialistic impulse. Characters must choose between survival, implying the acceptance of money and therefore of existing moral and social standards, and freedom, which rejects ethics and finances together. Judy's final line . . . is a first step to total freedom through anarchy. There can be no question of these two societies — the materialistic and the anarchic — coexisting. In Brenton's typical fashion, the political problems are raised but not solved. . . .

To read the play naturalistically without seeing the larger juxtaposition of the everyday and the darkly primal is dangerous; the theme of wife-beating, for example, then assumes disproportionate importance, and the lurid violence is reduced to mere psychological expression. Brenton, the man of political conviction, is examining issues of far greater scope and uses violence only in the service of larger social themes. . . . At times the play almost becomes a stark, subtle poem, infused with concentric images, yet the sheer theatricality of the story alone keeps the play continually dramatic.

Ben Cameron, 'Howard Brenton: The Privilege of Revolt',
Theater, Spring 1981, p. 32-3

The Romans in Britain

A play in two parts.
First production: Olivier Theatre, London, 16 Oct. 1980
(dir Michael Bogdanov).
Published: Methuen, 1980, 1981.

Part One, 'Caesar's Tooth', is set in London in 54 B.C. Two Celtic robbers 'on the run' encounter the three sons of a matriarchal clan, 'a family and its fields', who are threatened by a Roman invasion. One robber is killed, the other, Conlag, escapes. 'Two worlds touch' when the three sons encounter three Roman soldiers by the river, and two are killed by the Romans while the third, a Druid priest, Marban, is raped. Conlag meets a group of 'fugitives and refugees' of the Roman invasion, and Marban is captured by Caesar's army. Caesar extracts a troublesome tooth and orders Marban to wear a Venus medallion, so that he commits suicide, as 'The Gods Grow Small'. The first part ends with 'Two Murders', as Conlag is killed by the Celtic female slave he has abducted, and she is in turn killed by the British army, 'with the equipment of the late 1970s.' Part Two, 'Arthur's Grave', alternates between Ireland in 1980 and Britain in 515 A.D. In 'A Blunder', Thomas Chichester, a British Army officer, is hiding in a field disguised as an Irish freedom fighter, and is roughed up by British troops. Cai, a patriarchal forefather of Chichester, kills an invading Saxon soldier, and is himself killed by his daughters Corda and Morgana after 'A Soliloquy' from Chichester, who reveals he has 'A Contract' with a man called O'Rourke. Adona, 'The Last Roman Lady', is robbed and killed by her Steward and two Cooks. In 'An Execution', Chichester is killed by O'Rourke and his men. In the final scene, 'The Making of Arthur', Corda, Morgana and the two Cooks join forces and the First Cook, in his new guise as a priest, tells a story about King Arthur.

I thought it went beyond the bounds [of decency]. My wife covered her head during the sodomy scene . . . a disgrace to the National Theatre. Its staging shows a singular lack of judgment. . . . I have no doubt that the GLC will be considering its position vis-a-vis the National Theatre at an early date.

Sir Horace Cutler, Tory GLC leader,
in *The Evening Standard*, 17 Oct. 1980

The play is staged because we must maintain a commitment to the new as well as to the old. The fact that new writers today are often outspoken and provocative must not discourage us and Howard Brenton is a serious and important dramatist with an international reputation.

The Romans in Britain was very fully discussed at Monday's board meeting, at which I said I have complete faith in the integrity of the playwright, director, and the play. It is in my view an ambitious and remarkable piece of dramatic writing. . . . I nevertheless understand that some might find the play strong.

Sir Peter Hall, in *The Evening Standard*, 17 Oct. 1980

One is concerned about protecting the citizens, and in particular young people. I'm talking about men being so stimulated by the play that they will commit attacks on young boys.

Mrs. Mary Whitehouse, 17 Oct. 1980

. . . Homosexual rape, bloody violence, frequent obscenity and political signifying do not necessarily make for a mature play and so many of his parallels are driven home with a bludgeon that his regard for an adult audience must be questioned. . . . His idea of Celtic culture is more excremental than elemental, with the language largely drawn from references to bodily functions as an indication of the primitive level of society. . . .

Such key attempts at broadening the dramatic vocabulary of the English stage are necessary, and the National Theatre is the only place where such adventures can really be tried, but the play is riven with condescension for its audience. There are moments that work and ideas that deserve an airing, but there are so many misjudgments in the writing and the production that it is difficult to determine where things really went wrong.

Ned Chaillet, *The Times*, 17 Oct. 1980

. . . An epic play with only one idea in its head: that the invasion of Celtic Britain by Romans and Saxons bred in our ancestors inextinguishable dreams of empire manifested again today in Northern Ireland. But there is such a vast disproportion between the extravagances of the form and the banality of the thesis. . . . I accept totally that Mr. Brenton finds the hunger for empire anathema; but in order to savage such a crucial historical phenomenon I suggest you first have to understand it.

Michael Billington,
The Guardian, 17 Oct. 1980

Each time I see a new play by Howard Brenton I feel a slight sense of reassurance. Could *The Churchill Play* have been quite as appalling as I thought? Why, yes — here is *Sore Throats* to confirm my judgment. But suppose *Sore Throats* was really a little better than it seemed to me? Well, there is nothing in *The Romans in Britain* . . . to suggest any such thing. Its three hours are devoid of wit, beauty or drama, and the message it appears to offer us only surfaces in the closing scenes. Whatever weaknesses there may be in Mr. Brenton's writing, inconsistency isn't one of them.

B. A. Young,
The Financial Times, 18 Oct. 1980

What I call the Amadeus Defence works in the following way: you are concerned to forestall criticism of the strikingly bad play you are about to write; so you make the work as obscene as you can, with the result that any critic who objects to it lays himself open to charges of puritanism and narrow-mindedness. The aim is to make the general public say to itself: 'If we are having a perfectly horrible time, this must be in the cause of Great Art.'

What I call the Brenton Variation throws in left-wingery and the Irish dimension, so that the audience should feel: 'If, when we are not bored rigid by this play, we find it utterly repugnant, that is because we are imperialist pigs who do not care two hoots about the crimes the British Army is committing in our name.'

Neither the Defence nor the Variation should be effective against a little calm self-questioning. . . . Do we for instance care anything about the Celtic criminal who is strung up by the feet while his throat is cut? If the odd Roman soldier sodomized the odd Druid, what is that to us? Answer: nothing . . .

This play is a nauseating load of rubbish from beginning to end. It is written in a ludicrous pseudo-poetic yob-talk; such themes as it possesses are banal beyond belief; and the intended bravery of the acting company amounts to no more than an embarrassing exhibitionism.

It is advertised as unsuitable for children. It is unsuitable for anyone. If I were Sir Peter Hall and had instigated such a production, I would take myself out to dinner and very tactfully but firmly sack myself over the dessert.

James Fenton, *The Sunday Times*, 19 Oct. 1980

Mindful of our history, theatre-lovers must defend the right of playwrights, actors, directors, theatre managements and even reviewers to take risks and make mistakes. I happen to admire much of Brenton's work and to have published many of his plays. For me *The Romans in Britain* is a dramatic poem of considerable force and beauty. I think it will live in our theatre and grow in our minds: we owe the National Theatre a great debt for staging it. But those who have seen it or read it and think differently must be free to say so, passionately if need be.

What I hope can be agreed is that theatre workers and playgoers must make their own decisions and that threats of censorship, whether by Lord Chamberlain, local government or police, must be resisted.

Geoffrey Strachan, letter to *The Times*, 20 Oct. 1980

Having seen the scene, my opinion is that it would not be prosecutable. It would not induce anything in anybody except feelings of extreme horror and aversion.

John Mortimer QC, in *The Times*, 20 Oct. 1980

I feel that such an admirable and cogent case, too strong to be called a 'defence', put by Mr. Geoffrey Strachan (October 20) on behalf of Eyre Methuen, stands in supreme dignity, by itself, unfettered by less effective contributions.

Sir Laurence Olivier, letter to *The Times*, 22 Oct. 1980

I don't go to the theatre to see a lot of buggery. We get quite enough of that at home.

John Osborne, letter to *The Guardian*, 23 Oct. 1980

Horrified at the Roman's murderous exploitation of the people and mankind's general appetite for food, Brenton demonstrates that exploitation isn't just the copyright of rulers but of playwrights, too. He himself sets about exploiting murder. From the menu of human monstrosity, he serves up death by spear, sword and stone; homosexual and heterosexual rape; blood guzzling; but, avoiding one cliché of the avant-garde, not even a cannibalistic nibble unless you count the Centurion demanding of one pummelled Druid, 'Suck me off'. . . .

Newspaper headlines have made *The Romans in Britain* a subject of scandal and concern, giving an aura of excitement to an event that otherwise would have sunk under the weight of its own boredom. It would be wrong to think that the oafish public outcry means the play is either sensational or good. It is neither. Theatre is the art of sensation, being moved and made to feel; but Brenton's play is so sprawling, so devoid of tension or characterization that it is impossible to feel anything. Instead of being an antidote to barbarity, the play's artlessness adds to it by making an audience indifferent to the stage suffering.

John Lahr, 'The Cruelty of Theatre', *New Society*, 23 Oct. 1980

. . . the play's intellectual and political crudeness, its sentimental appeals to an Arthurian utopia and, sometimes, a lack of plausibility that lurches towards Pythonesque exorbitance . . .

Benedict Nightingale, 'Mailed Fist and Iron Heart',
New Statesman, 24 Oct. 1980

As for the fiasco at the Olivier, it is hard to understand why Howard Brenton occupies the quasi-official position that he does at the National; he has shown no sign of being able to write a play so far and the reiterated limitations of class confusion and socio-sexual immaturity are stridently boring. Michael Bryant as Caesar in Britain has to shout 'What a fucking island!' towards the end of the first act and most of us . . . I believe would have liked to yell back 'What a fucking play!' It is wrong of the GLC leader to wave a grant at the National as a warning, but equally irritating of the National to put critics in the position of having to defend in principle the poor practice of their pet young playwright.

Bryan Robertson, *The Spectator*, 25 Oct. 1980

I am not concerned with the issues of artistic standards, obscenity, indecency or dramatic politicking in themselves. My purpose was to question whether any production so lacking in redeeming features (and grossly offensive to boot) ought to be staged at public expense.

Sir Horace Cutler, letter to *The Times*, 26 Oct. 1980

I categorically deny that there is any scene in that play which is as revolting as what happens to Gloucester in *King Lear* or to Oedipus in *Oedipus Rex*. Yet even school children are quite justifiably urged to see these plays.

The Romans in Britain is a deeply serious play which reveals the conviction of its author, Howard Brenton, that the heart of man is desperately wicked, a conviction that has been held by many great and religious writers in the past, and the climax of its first act is as fine and thunderstriking as anything seen or heard on the London stage for a very long time.

Sir Harold Hobson, letter to *The Times*, 29 Oct. 1980

Whatever the dubious alliance of Sir Horace Cutler and Mrs. Mary Whitehouse may have led you to believe, the scandal of *The Romans in Britain* ... has nothing at all to do with naked Romans and Celts going up each other like knives, nor yet to do with theatrical censorship. The scandal here concerns an artistic director engaged abroad when he could or at least should have been expecting trouble at home, and more importantly the artistic administration of a state-subsidized company which could allow this play to get beyond the Xerox machine, let alone into first rehearsal. Not because it is scandalous, or tasteless, or shocking, but because it is an underwritten and overproduced pageant which would look inadequate if performed as a school play.

Sheridan Morley, 'Museum Piece', *Punch*, 29 Oct. 1980

Over the past 20 years English playwriting has been good. Most English drama criticism has been bad. I think that must be beyond reasonable dispute. One piece of dry land in troubled waters....

Our right-wing Establishments desperately need 'culture': it is their justification for ruling the 'uncultured mob'. They see it as what stands between them and the barbaric consequences of their economic and social programmes. It is the figleaf they put on when they look at themselves in the mirror....

So it is that in recent years the English right-wing Establishment have put money into our most successful cultural institution — the theatre — while its best dramatists have passionately experimented in the creation of socialist art. . . .

Of course not all dramatists are socialists. Beckett is said to have made liberal — even capitalist — culture possible. He is said to have shown that however you degrade people an unquenchable spark of humanity remains in them — and therefore we are not animals but may still hope to build a humane society. . . .

Most dangerous of all is the teaching of culture in our universities. There Beckett and the Absurdists still often stand for high art. Where can the young turn for answers, when the dignity of human intelligence is so often not respected even in our universities?

The theatre is one of our few vital institutions. It has been comparatively free from censorship: free, that is, to explore human and social relations to a degree often denied other media. . . .

And so we come to the wreckers. Horace Cutler is leader of the GLC. Recently he left the National Theatre in a rage (at least I hope it wasn't his normal behaviour) and in a cable to its artistic director threatened to cut its funds. (I hope he paid for the cable.) . . . Cutler speaks in a gentleman's voice and behaves and dresses as a gentleman. Dramatists know that clothes and accents make good disguises . . . if (say) a politician may use certain words to describe the conduct of one man, it is important that we use the same words to describe the same conduct (however disguised) of another man. With this in mind we may safely describe Horace Cutler as a lout and a hooligan.

He openly — and apparently without remorse, since so far as I know he has not apologized — attacked the freedom of the theatre. The *Sunday Times* thought a resignation was called for — not, as you might think, of Horace Cutler but Peter Hall! . . . Some of us, if we were Mr. Fenton, would jump in the river. . . .

Mr. Fenton's article was one of the most ugly, superficial and hysterical bits of criticism I've seen — a yowlp straight out of Yahoo-Land. I have been a dramatist for some 18 years. My plays have been prosecuted by the police and frequently attacked by the critics. I make no claim for them except that they have survived to receive more generous, and perhaps more adequate, attention . . . I don't know what credentials Mr. Fenton has for his job, I have just stated one of mine. Relying on that I now call on Mr. Fenton to resign. I can tell him . . . that he does not understand the new theatre and so is not fit to write about it. . . .

Many people would like to see the end of political theatre. They might as well want the end of politics in newspapers. Theatre is about our lives. Writers in all creative ages of drama have known that man is a political animal in the very foundations of his behaviour, consciousness and morality. Shakespeare, Euripides, Molière — all were intensely political. The ancient dramatic injunction 'Know thyself!' is political.

> Edward Bond, 'The Romans and the Establishment's Fig Leaf',
> *The Guardian*, 3 Nov. 1980

I suspect that if ever the kind of 'freedom' [Bond] writes about reaches Britain, it will be hard to find good newspapers like *The Guardian*, or good theatres like the National, or good dramatists like Edward Bond, or good critics like James Fenton. Though I have no qualifications for saying so.

> Jeremy Treglown, letter to *the Guardian*, 5 Nov. 1980

I venture to suggest that Beckett, in his work, remains as human in his concerns as Bond and, although he may or may not be a 'socialist dramatist', knows as much about the monster in man as Bond does.

> Harold Pinter, letter to *The Guardian*, 5 Nov. 1980

I personally have no wish to judge what others should see. What I do question is what comes next. Are we to see child molestation — simulated or real — perhaps to symbolize the rape of the Third World by the colonial powers? Or defecation — to show contempt for materialism?

Perhaps we could have necrophilia, with real live corpses!

> Sir Horace Cutler, letter to *The Guardian*, 8 Nov. 1980

Brenton's play comes far closer to the sado-masochistic, pornographic literature of Soho than anything found in any English or Greek classic.

> Milton Shulman, letter to *The Guardian*, 12 Nov. 1980

Bond has attacked Fenton, nibbling Beckett on the way; Pinter has attacked Bond for a foul on Beckett; Hampton has attacked Pinter while defending, with the aid of Brecht, Bond's defence of Brenton. Osborne is ribald from the sideline. If this is to be a free-for-all among the pros, may I add my pennorth? . . .

Because a writer feels he is on the right side politically and morally, the words he uses will not therefore take care of themselves. The only way he has of examining the truth of his thoughts is to examine the truth of his language. If he does this insufficiently he neglects the talent which is his main excuse for being listened to. . . . After all, one of the most entertaining and least po-faced of the letters in the series has been by the unqualified Horace Cutler. Right, who's next?

> James Saunders, letter to *The Guardian*, 14 Nov. 1980

. . . Sir Horace's sense of humour. Having asserted that 'your typical worker' (sic) doesn't want to hear or see 'effing and blinding or sodomy' on stage, he speculates as to whether 'sexual congress with animals as a parable of the class war' will come next. Who does he see as the animals, I wonder? And who does he see getting screwed?

> Steve Gooch, letter to *The Guardian*, 14 Nov. 1980

I only write letters to the newspapers these days in order to point out that I never write letters to the newspapers. I have, however, a couple of namesakes who do. . . . So when Mr. Saunders . . . takes me to task, his finger is unfortunately pointing sternly in the wrong direction. . . . Since I haven't yet seen the play, I have nothing to say: except, of course, that a writer of Howard Brenton's obvious talent and integrity should never have been subjected to such torrents of mindless abuse; nor do I see why his play should be turned into a ping-pong ball for other people's theories.

> Christopher Hampton, letter to *The Guardian*, 18 Nov 1980

The Romans in Britain is a very good play indeed. . . . From the outset Mr. Brenton faced one very difficult problem; to find appropriate language for his Celts, Druids, Romans and Dark Age Britons. Many historical plays have foundered upon this rock, but Mr. Brenton skirts it with ease and grace. . . . Conjuring up an era that is culturally as well as historically remote is a notoriously difficult task for a playwright or novelist, but Mr. Brenton achieves it with great skill and effect. . . .

The rape scene is handled with a casual certainty that robs it of all offence except to those determined to be offended and those . . . who have been secretly disappointed to find that it is in no way titillating or salacious, let alone sexually arousing. It is fully justified in its context, written with obvious dramatic and moral honesty, and in any case brief; it is also horribly plausible, which I think settles the argument, and settles it in favour of the author.

> Bernard Levin, 'Conquered by the Romans on the South Bank',
> *The Times*, 11 March 1981

On rare occasions, the yelps of the puritanical help focus public attention on what might be termed 'breakthrough' art — i.e., art that moves society up the evolutionary aesthetic ladder. But all too often, as in the case here, such attention merely illuminates the second-rate. The furor over *The Romans in Britain* was pretty much the making of a mountain out of a molehill. . . .

What *The Romans in Britain* did was to provide the means for various groups and individuals to argue points, most of which had little to do with the play and a great deal to do with the precarious economic/ political/moral state in which the British nation now finds itself.

Bernard Weiner, 'The *Romans in Britain* Controversy', p. 68

Since 1968 a number of quite violent and provocative plays, as well as works with explicit sexual activity of ever description, have appeared regularly on the British stage. That none was engulfed in anything like the level of controversy surrounding *The Romans* is surely due in part to the play's content, a confluence of controversial subjects remarkable in a single work. . . . What sparked off and sustained the critics' fire in this case was that, by virtue of being presented at the National Theatre . . . *The Romans* was seen by some as striking deeply at the nation's honour and values not only because of its subject matter, but because the thing was perpetrated within the cultural Holy of Holies. 'We are worried that the National is lending respectability to the play', complained Mrs. Whitehouse; and many others were distressed that the play tarnished the prestige of the National. . . . It may well turn out that the ultimate and unwelcome legacy of *The Romans* will not be a change in moral or artistic or political consciousness, but a less tolerant attitude towards the National Theatre itself, which brought forth and nurtured Brenton's invasion.

Richard Beacham, 'Brenton Invades Britain', p. 37

Brenton's play is one of the most important contributions for many years to what he sees as the long-standing disgrace of the British in Ireland. Whatever the nature of individual political opinion, that it should be dismissed overnight by drama critics and be the subject of attempted persecution, not on the grounds that its premises are false (since there's been little or no analysis of the play in these terms) but on the grounds that it incites to buggery, is an insult to a serious writer. While we treat our writers in this fashion, nothing will be resolved.

Philip Roberts, 'Howard Brenton's Romans', p. 21

Brenton's special achievement as a post-Brechtian writer may be more apparent in . . . *The Romans in Britain* . . . which is currently on trial for 'sexual offences' in London. . . . One suspects that the court case against Brenton and the National Theatre represents conservative distress at the political implications of his epic history, as well as its sexual violence. Brenton sees ancient and recent British history in far less flattering terms than many historians; but then the others were not usually writing from an anti-imperialistic perspective. In a sense Brenton is *changing* history by writing it anew, and this too may have provoked the outcry against his play. . . . Now he has managed to intervene in history, or at least in public discourse with one of his plays, and the British court system has practically become Brenton's co-producer.

Joel Schechter, 'Beyond Brecht: New Authors, New Spectators', in John Fuegi *et al.*, eds, *Beyond Brecht: Brecht Yearbook Vol. 1*, (Detroit: Wayne State University Press, 1983), p. 46-7

Bertolt Brecht would have laughed about the trial of *The Romans in Britain*. The irony of the prosecuting counsel withdrawing on his own initiative produced something very like the 'improvised justice' dispensed by Brecht's ramshackle judge, Azdak, in *The Caucasian Chalk Circle*. . . .

Libertarians have to some degree been frightened away from discussing how to stop sexual exploiters because of the right-wing diversion Mrs. Whitehouse has fronted for a decade or more. I think her influence is about to wane. Now male socialists and libertarians, learning not from Mary Whitehouse but from the women's movement, must sort out where they stand on the difference between sexual liberation and sexual exploitation. Feminists are doing far more than Mrs. Whitehouse has ever done to stop the sexual abuse in our daily life.

The only court a moral campaigner, or indeed a playwright, needs is somewhere to be heard — a theatre — the only jury, an audience there of its own free will. The only judgment worth having, for moralist or storyteller, is to be believed. All Mary Whitehouse had to do was to challenge me, the true 'procurer' of *The Romans in Britain*, to a public debate. She never communicated with me, she never saw the play. We could have gone on television or onto the Olivier stage. But instead she tried to cut out my tongue, by trying to outlaw my play and trying to break my director's hands on a legal rack of her own design.

Howard Brenton, 'Who Will Judge Our Morality?', *New Statesman*, 2 Apr. 1982

I remember Edward Bond . . . when he came down to see *The Romans in Britain* (like a fire engine in full cry, to sort the trouble out!) . . . said that if we took all the gags out of the show, we'd have a piece of highly acceptable 'art'. Why we were in trouble, he said, was because of the gags coming off the stage. Particularly in what became known as 'the rape scene'. To the Roman soldiers that incident is a minor irritation, on a bad afternoon, a long way from home in a backwater of the empire. . . . The backlash of the scene, what horrifies, is its casualness. The soldiers joke as they murder and bungle a rape. It's obscene. I have never said anything other than that the scene is about a vile obscenity. I think it's true to what happens in war. . . . Since I wrote the play, I've been to a battle zone — West Beirut, during the Israeli siege in the summer of 1981. The play . . . well, it's sort of true, though very pale and inadequate. It was very odd to find myself discussing *The Romans in Britain* with a PLO Officer one night in that city, during an air-raid.

Brenton, 'The Red Theatre under the Bed', p. 198

Thirteenth Night

'A dream play' in nineteen scenes.

First production: by the Royal Shakespeare Company at the Warehouse, London 2 July 1981 (dir. Barry Kyle; with Michael Pennington as Beaty). *Broadcast:* as Radio Four's Monday Play, 28 Nov. 1983 (dir. Michael Hefferman; with Tom Wilkinson as Beaty).

Published: Thirteenth Night and A Short Sharp Shock! (Methuen, 1981).

Jack Beaty, a left-wing leader of a Labour Party ward, is hit on the head during a fight with fascist thugs after a party meeting. He dreams the rest of the play, a version of Macbeth *set in contemporary Britain. Egged on by his mistress, Jenny Gaze, Jack kills the Labour Prime Minister, Bill Dunn, with a fire axe, and takes over the country. He has a fellow Cabinet member, Feast, eliminated, while Murgatroyd, a drunken MacDuff figure, drowns in his Californian swimming pool. Beaty mistakes the Ambassador from Chad for Banquo at Chequers, and in a bunker beneath Whitehall he is confronted with the ghosts of his victims together with Stalin, before being discovered as a withered corpse by three female anarchist witch-figures. In the play's Epilogue we see him walking along a beach, with a lame leg and a stick, recalling his dream to Jenny.*

Thirteenth night, the night after twelfth night, when the celebrations have to stop . . . I get sick of plays about the left, which do not mention the basic socialist problem. I mean — the blood in the Revolution's cradle. It's about Stalinism. A class war is a civil war. You need a secret police to win it, but then . . . how do you get rid of your secret police? You're into 'state capitalism', that curious form of autocracy which has haunted socialist history. Weighty stuff! All the nightmares of my

comrades. . . . There was a private reason for writing *Thirteenth Night*.
I discussed state oppression with a group of dissidents in, as they say,
'an Eastern European country'. I promised to write a play for them.
Thirteenth Night was it. After the RSC production it was broadcast by
BBC Radio 4. I'm certain they heard it.

Brenton, 'The Red Theatre under the Bed', p. 200

After *The Romans in Britain* he has not exactly abandoned historical
parallels and precedents for *Thirteenth Night*, but instead of casting the
play in the mould of the past he has pushed it ahead in time, making it a
sort of future fiction. We are past the time when Mr. Brenton could be
called a promising playwright; his general stage mastery is increasingly
obvious and there is a profligate display of it in the new play. . . .

There is much ingenuity in Mr. Brenton's exploitation of Shakespeare,
and it goes beyond his skilful echoing of famous lines. He sets the
characters of Shakespeare to find the elements in the British character
which could transform an Englishman into a Stalin, and closes in on his
creation with an overall wit to match his horror. . . . The comedy is
harsh, and the aim of the work is high. While Mr. Brenton projects an
absolutist state of the left, it is clearly not his intention to attack the left
politically. His concerns are with democratic participation and justice.

Ned Chaillet, 'Thirteenth Night', *The Times*, 6 July 1981

In a sense, *Macbeth* is a lure and a snare for Brenton, because it inveigles
him into concentrating on the internal corruption of Beaty as, like his
tartan forbear, he steps so far in blood that returning were as tedious as
go o'er. His emphasis as a dramatist has hitherto been the present state
and future prospects of Britain itself, and I, for one, felt puzzled and
mildly swindled by his cursory treatment of a subject so obviously
congenial to him and relevant to the rest of us. What's going on outside
Beaty's Stalinist eyrie, in the factories, the banks, the working men's
clubs, the police stations, the streets? . . . Brenton can, of course, argue
that this is a 'dream', and therefore bound to be substantially personal
and subjective; but that only leaves one wondering if the dream was
worth chronicling in the first place. Shakespeare has already said most of
what needs to be said about the evolution of Beaty as individual and
archetype.

Benedict Nightingale, 'Poor Players', *New Statesman*, 10 July 1981

. . . a dreary political fable which began life on the stage and should have
ended it there. . . . The play consists chiefly as a dream — always good
radio material. . . . It all added up to a laborious, rather unpleasant

drama, full of political argument — sometimes rather vividly phrased — and eruptions of violent action. Interesting chiefly as an insight into the preoccupations and delusions of the socialist mind, the play delivered the lumpen message that power corrupts and means shape ends. No doubt there are lefties around who need reminding of this, and it is nice of Mr. Brenton to take the trouble, but really I think Shakespeare put it rather better.

Nigel Andrew, 'Tomorrow and Tomorrow', *The Listener*, 8 Dec. 1983

The Genius

A two act play.
First production: Royal Court Theatre, London, 8 Sept. 1983
(dir. Danny Boyle).
First American production: Mark Taper Forum Theater, Los Angeles,
30 Apr. 1984 (dir. Ben Levit).
Published: Methuen Royal Court Writers Series, 1983.

Brenton tells the story of Leo, a top American government mathematician seconded to an obscure British university as a penalty for concealing his findings from the Pentagon. On the campus, he encounters a brilliant first-year student who has reached the same conclusions without understanding their fatal significance. To her, the equations are beauty itself; when he explains that they spell the end of the world she enters into a state of deranged agony that persists for the rest of the play.

Meanwhile, news of the discovery is spreading around, involving the abrupt abduction of the Bursar by MI5 and an offer from the Soviet Union delivered by the university's resident mole; and a final squaring of the balance of terror before Leo and the girl join forces in an air-base demonstration.

Irving Wardle, 'Campus Equations', *The Times*, 13 Sept. 1983

While I was working on the Brecht, I thought — what would a twentieth century Galileo be? I wanted to write a play on the Galileo theme for the National's smaller house, the Cottesloe, to run alongside the Brecht in the Olivier. But this megalomanic scheme came to nothing. *The Genius*, which I originally called *The Galileo's Goose*, got written and performed at the Royal Court three years later. I thought that a modern Galileo

Galilei would be an American, brilliant, glamorous, spoilt — what the Americans like to call 'emotionally developed', that is, a bit of a shit. In a way, his brilliance is a curse. He can't handle its consequences, the research he blundered into. The plot of the play turns on the question 'who will teach the teacher?' That's why I called him Leo Lehrer. He ends up becoming the student of one of his students.

Brenton, 'The Red Theatre under the Bed', p. 200

As a dramatist I try to get stories going where something huge — like a new scientific discovery which will affect the arms race horribly — which is bouncing on the poor heads of some very second-rate people who aren't doing very well in a rather grotty university in England. I show people trying to deal with history, and getting smashed up. My characters are often around a cusp, and suddenly find themselves with a torch in their hands, which they realize is world history, and they drop it. Comic writing often comes out of that. It's an attempt at a macro-micro view.

Brenton, Address at University of New South Wales, Australia, 23 May 1984

Although it makes a lot of other recent theatrical contributions to the nuclear debate look puny and is unashamed of ideas, it finally lapses into emotional rhetoric. . . . Brenton sets the stage for a moral debate. . . . But then, having devised a brilliant situation . . . blows it by lapsing into political melodrama. . . . It is a pity because Brenton is on to big ideas in this play. Is pure research possible in industrially-sponsored science departments? Is there a frightening scientific ignorance in people who hold political and academic power? And, above all, at what point morally does the scientist sever responsibility for his discoveries? But although it is refreshing to hear such ideas even aired on the British stage, it would be even better to hear them debated.

Michael Billington, 'Dangers in Being Too Clever by Half', *The Guardian*, 13 Sept. 1983

His wonderful new play at the Royal Court takes up the theme of an innovator's responsibility in the nuclear age and achieves an astonishing lift off into the related realms of education, the Cold War, student radicalism and political theory. *The Genius* is rich in pertinent argument, dense with beautifully hard and mobile characterization, teeming with memorable stage pictures, and bristling with Brenton's very best writing: flinty, impassioned, explosive.

Michael Coveney, *Financial Times*, 13 Sept. 1983

Like all Brenton's plays, *The Genius* is written in the broad, decisive strokes of a poster artist. Argument, character, narrative short-cuts, shock tactics, all come together with the aim of making an unambiguous statement with the maximum force. But unless the play is merely restating the well-rehearsed nuclear litany on power, intellectual betrayal, and the corruption of science, its meaning (not to mention its plotting) is extremely elusive.

> Irving Wardle, 'Campus Equations', *The Times*, 13 Sept. 1983

Writing in the nuclear world, which was just accessible to Brecht (who indeed made changes to the original text of *Galileo* in reaction to the testing of the first atomic bomb), Brenton has turned the earlier writer's conclusion on its head. The crime of Brecht's scientist was his recantation in the face of the Inquisition, thus denying science the possibility of public access. That of Lehrer is to have looked in the first place.

> John Bull, *New British Political Dramatists*, p. 220

Bloody Poetry

A two act play, commissioned by Foco Novo Theatre Company.
First production: Haymarket Theatre, Leicester, 1 Oct. 1984,
    transferring to Hampstead Theatre, London, 31 Oct. 1984
    (dir. Roland Rees).
First American production: Manhattan Theatre Club at City Center
    Theater, New York, 26 December 1986 (dir. Lynne Meadow).
Published: Methuen, 1985.

Partly based on Richard Holmes's book Shelley: The Pursuit.
Act One is set on the shores of Lake Geneva in 1816, where Bysshe, Mary Shelley and Claire Clairemont, who is the lover of both Bysshe and Lord Byron, meet up with the latter. Claire declares she wants to be 'loved, happy and free', and Byron proposes they 'go Communist'. The group read, discuss and write poetry and play games, observed by John Polidori, Byron's biographer and a narrator figure in the play. Claire falls pregnant to Byron, and Bysshe and Byron go out in a boat on the lake in a storm, where Bysshe declares he cannot swim.

In Act Two, Bysshe's wife Harriet, who has become a prostitute and is pregnant, drowns herself in the Serpentine. Mary and Bysshe get married, but are refused custody of Bysshe's two children. They leave with Claire for Italy, accompanied by Harriet's ghost. Bysshe and Claire go to Venice to see Byron, who has sent his and Claire's daughter Allegra to a convent, where she later dies. Byron refuses to see Claire, but takes Bysshe to a madhouse. Bysshe and Mary's daughter dies in Venice while he is writing a poem about the Peterloo massacre. Shelley's death by drowning at La Spezia is contrasted with his poem 'The Triumph of Life'.

Bloody Poetry is a companion piece to my play *Sore Throats*. They are personal plays. What Byron and Shelley and their friends and lovers tried to do was to invent a new kind of family life. They failed, but I love them for their failure. It's a Utopian play. The characters are all, in their different ways, emotional and sexual voyagers. They had a conviction, which they couldn't really define, that there is a different way of living . . . just out of reach. There's a third play to write out of this.

Brenton, 'The Red Theatre under the Bed', p. 199

Partly the play is a feverish, dream-like evocation of the political and sexual radicalism of Byron and Shelley. But it is also, and this is what makes it interesting, an exploration of the relative impotence of poetry in achieving revolution. . . .

Brenton is, in fact, doing something markedly ambitious in this phantasmagoric play. He is celebrating the idea of the committed artist who seeks to stir and provoke sullen, defeated bourgeois England. At the same time, with clear-eyed honesty, he shows how difficult it is to upset the moral order. . . . He also reminds one that while poets talk people are massacred at Peterloo and that the 'unacknowledged legislators' are often far from the distant thunder of action.

Michael Billington, *The Guardian*, 6 Nov. 1984

How odd that a work of such feminist intent should fall so flat — but the difficulty is clear: Brenton wants to write about men's inability to see women's lives as real, but he can't write the women's roles fully. . . . We see nothing through the women's eyes, so the children's deaths are just mechanical. Not only do the women talk less than the men when everyone's together — that's natural enough — they don't say much or do much when they're by themselves. Brenton seems unable to imagine them, proving his thesis but ruining his play.

Erika Munk, 'Every Poet in His Kind',
Village Voice, 20 Jan. 1987, p. 86

c: Film

Skinflicker

41 mins. Made by Portable Films in 1972.
Directed by Tony Bicât, produced by the British Film Institute,
    photographed by Christopher Phillips (with Will Knightley,
    William Hoyland, and Henry Woolf).
Unpublished.

Partly based on the Laporte kidnapping in Canada. A study of the repressive backlash to a misguided but sympathetically presented act of terrorism. 'A teacher, a nurse and a garrulous layabout kidnap a public man somewhere in England. They employ a cameraman, a maker of blue films, to record what happens. The story ends with the defection of the cameraman, the murder of the public man, and the suicide of the kidnappers. At a later date the material shot for the film is edited by government officials for '"training" purposes, to instruct public employees in the mores of extremist groups. It is in this form that the story is told.'

Synopsis from Brenton's script

I think the ideas in the piece were in some way wrong. It was too enclosed. If you're going to make a dialectical piece, it has to be much dirtier, of a much wider stature. . . . And, though artistically it was neat, in terms of getting anywhere near the real world it was far too linear, two-dimensional. That's something I've tried to get over with *Magnificence*. . . . I thought the revolutionaries in *Skinflicker* were dangerously heroic.

Brenton, 'Messages First', p. 24-5

There's an interesting idea somewhere in Howard Brenton's script, but it's drowned in the film's muddied waters. It's clear, for instance, that the use of a blue film-maker parodies the notion of audience (silent majority?) as voyeurs of the pornography of violence. But the idea needs a framework, a structure to enable us to differentiate the film's farrago of style and methods. . . .

The confusion is only compounded by references to actual events . . . which undermine the film's repeated reminders of illusion. . . . If you're going to use a Brechtian device, it's worth recalling that one of Brecht's most effective distancing devices was something as simple as a chalk line. . . . *Skinflicker* is an intellectual conceit, and a hollow one.

David Wilson, 'My Childhood and *Skinflicker*',
Sight and Sound, Spring 1973, p. 115

Skinflicker is already well on the way to being established as a 'controversial' film, yet exactly what it is trying to say might prove a more substantial subject for polemic than whether it should be allowed to say it. The film's obvious strength lies in the raw immediacy which it achieves from making its technical shortcomings part of its plot. . . . We are left . . . as voyeurs to an act of violence, yet cheated of the context which would enable us, if not to judge then at least to understand either the act or our own voyeurism. The gap between the angry and the powerful is already large enough off the screen, and the 'artistic' distortions employed to emphasize it here serve primarily to distance us from any responsibility for it.

Jan Dawson, *Monthly Film Bulletin*, March 1973, p. 58

d. Television Plays

Lushly

A 30 minute play.
First transmitted: BBC2 Thirty Minute Theatre, 21 Aug. 1972
   (dir. Brian Farnham)
Unpublished.

A political exploration of the relationship between three workmen — Jim and Bag, both housepainters, and their foreman Eddy — and their employer and his cynical agent. While the workmen are redecorating a dilapidated slum house, Jim attempts to complain to the owner of the house, Hardacre, about Eddy's alcoholism. When he finally gets to see Hardacre, the latter is cavorting James Bond-style in a bath with naked secretaries. The three workers go to a pub, where they meet a deposed military governor from Venezuela. They return to the house with bottles of spirits and a crate of beer, and are merrily splashing paint around the place when the owner's agent enters.

Had refreshingly crisp and nasty bits . . . though its characters were a trifle heavily etched. The villain, for instance, had burned budgies as a boy, and sexually assaulted the family's Yorkshire terrier. . . . His efficient viciousness was meant to contrast cruelly with the sottish shambling decency of two house-painters he employs. . . . But fairly orthodox views about the beer-swilling idleness of the working class, which the villain would have heartily endorsed, seemed to be floating around just under the surface of the play's modish exchanges. The last scene, with the decorators dousing one another in white emulsion, confirmed that we were not in the theatre of the absurd but in custard-pie land.

John Carey, 'The Vanishing Partridge', *The Listener*, 31 Aug. 1972

There was exceptional energy in the language, there was blood between the lines of the rapid, tough jokes.

Adrian Mitchell, 'Funnies', *New Statesman*, 1 Sept. 1972

A Saliva Milkshake

30 minute play, adapted from Joseph Conrad's *Under Western Eyes*.
First transmitted: BBC2 'Eleventh Hour', 5 Jan. 1975
    (dir. Robert Knights). *Performed as a stage play:* at the Soho Poly
    Lunchtime Theatre, 23 June 1975 (dir. Robert Walker, with Dudley
    Sutton as Rafferty).
Published: in *Plays for the Poor Theatre* and by TQ Publications,
    1977. Also in *Performing Arts Journal*, Vol. III, No. 3 (Winter 1979).

The dilemma of a liberal intellectual caught in the crossfire of a political crisis which forces him to make a commitment. The English Home Secretary has been assassinated. Martin, a Cambridge graduate, arrives home to find Joan, an old college friend, in his flat. She tells him she is the assassin, and persuades him to collect a forged passport for her. Bearing in mind that he is in line for a Chair in Science, Martin tells his tutor about Joan, and is cajoled into complicity with Special Branch in setting a trap for her. She shoots herself, and Martin, who narrates the play, has his eardrums pierced by her comrades.

Written originally for the BBC's instant drama-journalism programme . . . By the time the play finally got shown, however, the point and purpose of the original brief scarcely applied . . . though the piece stands satisfactorily in its own right . . . As an exposé of the two-edged, two-faced mechanisms of the British Establishment the play worked well. . . . In spite of . . . actuality, however, the story remains slightly fantastical and inconsistent in places, its real continuity lying in the head of its central character, Martin.

Steve Gooch, 'Soho Poly Summer Season',
Plays and Players, Oct. 1975, p. 28

The Paradise Run

First transmitted: Thames TV 'Plays for Britain', 6 Apr. 1976
(dir. Michael Apted; with Ian Charleson).
Unpublished.

Two British soldiers, serving in Northern Ireland, find their lives cross. A young private, at a loss in the Army, is befriended by an officer. The private deserts to Sweden. The officer, on leave in London, has a crisis of conscience and decides to follow the private. Arriving in Stockholm, thinking he is joining an idealistic underground of escapees, he finds the private has gone to pieces and is drinking himself to death. Their run to a foreign paradise, out of the hell of serving in Northern Ireland, is an illusion.

Brenton, letter to Tony Mitchell, 2 Dec. 1986

It was an upsetting and unnerving exhibition of mental derangement. . . . Madness and near-mad fantasy can often be a cue for a string of vulgar and meaningless images of the Ken Russell kind, but only once, for a brief moment, does Brenton's play slip into that kind of cliché, when the officer, drunk on the floor, dreams of being buried up to his neck in sand with a mirage of a tray of Scotch, soda and ice appearing followed by a skeleton on a bed. For the rest, the alarm and the panic in the minds of confused heads is startling, leaving the viewer dazed by uncertainty.

Polly Toynbee, 'Case for a Black Mark', *The Observer*, 11 April 1976

Desert of Lies

An 85 minute play.
First transmitted: BBC1, 13 March 1984 (dir. Piers Haggard).
Unpublished.

Desert of Lies *employs an elaborate visionary structure in which the exploits of a group of nineteenth-century colonialists — a band of English missionaries who disappeared in the Kalahari Desert in 1848 — are dreamt across the attempts of a group of their latter-day counterparts — a small 1983 journalistic-cum-touristic expedition — to retrace their steps and discover what happened to them. . . . One of them, a scientific rationalist with a drink problem, played with typically slurred relish by Tom Bell, even talks about his loss of faith in terms of 'the future breaking out in me like a fever'. His modern-day equivalent — Cherie Lunghi's experience-hungry journalist — drinks only Diet Pepsi but she, too, eventually loses her faith in the desert, which is of course as much a state of mind as a place on a map. The state of mind in question is that classic colonialist combo: guilt masquerading as liberal concern. . . . What one of the black characters calls this 'prurient' interest in Africa is stunningly inverted by Brenton when he has a group of Namibian tribesmen voyeuristically observe Lunghi and her colleagues edging closer to death after their Land-Rover has broken down. Brenton has also rewritten Conrad here, inasmuch as it is the tribesmen who end up saving her from resorting to cannibalism in order to stay alive.*

Michael Poole, 'Lie Detector', *The Listener*, 8 Mar. 1984

Our experience of TV is intimate, alone or with maybe one or two

others, before a small screen with the curtains drawn. It seems to me to
be private, even secretive, whereas the press, and academics, call it a
mass medium. The TV plays I've written . . . are much more difficult
than the stage plays — more poetic and odd. A play like *Desert of Lies*
is pretty weird!

Brenton, 'The Red Theatre under the Bed', p. 196

Even after his excursion into Roman Britain, Brenton is still much
preoccupied with the question of imperialism. Satellites, he implies,
police the Third World as effectively as any gunboat ever did; and those
who work in the media, whether they recognize it or not, are the new
colonialists. . . .

Brenton's attempt to give this visionary scenario greater political edge
by mapping a third element across its concerns — the mostly off-camera
struggle of SWAPO guerrillas against South Africa — is far from
convincing. The same has to be said of the hi-tech dénouement and its
apparent dependence on the frankly racist notion of 'going native'. But
then, Brenton has never been exactly renowned for the subtlety of his
plotting. His strength has been precisely his boldness, his willingness to
go for the largest of themes. And whatever else it fails to do, *Desert of
Lies* is nothing if not ambitious — in its startling use of the studio as a
desert, in its willingness to engage television in a non-naturalistic way
and in its sheer imaginative awkwardness. It is this kind of ambition that
has been singularly lacking in the BBC's drama output of late.

Michael Poole, 'Lie Detector', *The Listener*, 8 Mar. 1984

Dead Head

A four-part, four-hour thriller series.
First transmitted: on BBC2, 15, 22, 29 Jan., and 5 Feb. 1986
(dir. Robert Walker; with Denis Lawson as Eddie, George Baker as
Eldridge, Lindsay Duncan as Mrs. Cass, Simon Callow as Hugo,
Norman Beaton as Caractacus, and Susannah Bunyan as Jill).
Published: Methuen, 1987.

*In Episode One, 'Why Me?', Eddie Cass, 'a hero of our time',
is given a package to deliver to an address by a Special Branch
agent in a pub in Peckham. He finds no one at the address, and
opens the package, to discover a hat box with a severed
woman's head inside it, which he throws into the Thames. He is*

subsequently arrested and charged with murder, as the hat box belonged to his ex-wife. But he is given £1,000 and a bottle of whisky and set free. In Episode Two, 'Anything for England', Eddie sees the Special Branch agent Hugo on a train and pursues him, only to end up handcuffed to him. The two men break into a country house and go into hiding. Later Eddie is shown slides of a dismembered corpse, 'a definitive map of every conceivable male desire', and realizes that MI5 are protecting the murderer, who they claim is Eddie's ex-wife's lover. Eddie is kept a prisoner, padlocked to a bed in Shropshire, and tortured. But Hugo is machine-gunned by two frogmen, who give Eddie a bag of money. In Episode Three, 'The War Room', Eddie is staying in a derelict house in Birmingham when he finds out his West Indian ex-flatmate Caractacus is in Bristol. Eddie searches for him and finds him dressed like a prince in a pool room. Caractacus starts Eddie on a fitness course in a black music gymnasium. They attempt to track down Stoker, the man who gave Eddie the parcel, but Caractacus reveals that he is a 'public servant' and is shot by a black woman. In Episode Four, 'The Patriot', Caractacus is identified as the 'sex horror killer' and his death stated as suicide. Eddie deliberately gets himself arrested in London, but is thrown out of prison. The headless woman's body is found on Barnes Common. Eldridge, one of the MI5 agents, finally whispers in Eddie's ear the name of the real murderer, but we do not hear it. Eddie promises to keep silent. In the final scene, we see him together with his ex-wife at a beach holiday resort.

With *Dead Head*, I wanted my central character, Eddie Cass, to talk directly to some unknown, lonely stranger in the great 'out there', in front of a telly screen somewhere in England. Eddie is never off the screen. There are lots of asides and voice-overs from him, and flash-back images from his memory. Everything is from his point of view. I tried to dramatize what I suspect many of those unknowable milions are feeling. Eddie doesn't know what on earth is going on, and who is doing what to him. The series is a shambolic quest in four parts to find out. Eddie does at the end, but he won't tell us! The Government buys him off. The name of the ultimate villain is whispered into his ear in the penultimate scene. We the viewers are excluded — as we, the citizens, are excluded from what goes on in the Cabinet Room, or MI5, or the judge's room at the back of an Old Bailey Court. Television is an ideal pornographic medium. That's why video nasties and video porn are so successful. Late at night, slip into a cassette. . . . TV is a vice. As a dramatist, that's why I like writing for it — I like its potential to be secretive and private, yet seen by millions.

Brenton, 'The Red Theatre under the Bed', p. 196-8

Dead Head . . . shot in super-murkovision, might have been designed to make the beetroot-and-acorn London of *Comrade Dad* seem appetizing. Here all are villains, most are nasty, and some are even patriots. . . . Bits of it were properly sinister; the main problem was with the tone, which hopped from straight-thriller to parody-thriller with no obvious awareness of the problems this set up. There were times when it all looked like a long commercial for some unguessable product — perhaps something to splash and cleanse the body with. . . .

As a thriller, *Dead Head* was up to its neck in trouble by the end of part one, and it closed with a double cop-out. First Eddie, who had spent three episodes being set up as a fall guy by the Government and the Special Branch . . . was mysteriously pardoned and paid off with a quarter of a million. Had the Establishment fried him, it would have been not only cheaper on the tax-payer, but also more plausible in terms of the paranoid plot. On top of this, one of the nobs then whispered in his ear (though it wasn't necessary) the name of the top-drawer sex-killer whom they were all protecting. 'Oh, oh well, in that case,' murmured Eddie gravely, '. . . Queen and Country'. We were meant, no doubt, to be set all a ponder about Palace delinquents.

Julian Barnes, *The Observer*, 19 Jan. and 9 Feb. 1986

Dead Head . . . is neither a pleasant thriller to watch nor to contemplate. Its characters are a particularly unsavoury lot. Its quotient of sex and violence is just about acceptable. Yet, there is no denying that it spins an intriguing tale, or that Howard Brenton knows how to find grim humour in the most unlikely places . . . a sinful world in which severed heads, official corruption and two-legged and four-legged scavengers are almost *de rigueur* . . . Brenton immersed himself in *film noirs* and old B-movies.

Peter Davalle, 'Dead Head', *The Times*, 15 Jan 1986

After accusations of 'TV Orgy' in the headlines of the popular press, it was with a mounting sense of expectation that one watched Howard Brenton's *Dead Head* . . . described by the BBC as 'an old style thriller for today'. . . . The narrative was deliberately close to parody, even if those elements of caricature were placed rather disconcertingly within some very realistic scenes from contemporary life.

The effect was like that of a comic strip brought violently to life: this gave a melodramatic edge to the proceedings. . . . Howard Brenton's script was at its best when it aspired to a sort of blank-verse cockney, combining lyricism with . . . whimsy; it was less effective, however, when it tried to make points about police corruption, racialism and so on. It is difficult to combine Gothic and polemic, even on television. . . .

Peter Ackroyd, 'Urban Grotesqueries', *The Times*, 16 Jan. 1986

Very few television programmes strive to expand the possibilities of a dominantly visual medium; *Dead Head* is one of those which can hold a candle to television commercials as a pictorial conception.

Celia Brayfield, 'Subliminal Images', *The Times*, 23 Jan. 1986

e: Adaptations

Gargantua

From Rabelais's novel.
First production: by the Brighton Combination in 1969.
Unpublished.

The idea of a huge giant swallowing people appealed to me. We begin to distort style. Two actors, for instance, look down at a doll's house. At the same time ten feet away there was a family sitting in an alcove — their house. The family start having Christmas dinner — when the two actors (the giants) over the doll's house suddenly announce: 'Look at those vermin!' and they take the roof off the doll's house. Then the actual family notice the roof coming off their house and DDT being sprayed in. The distortion of scales in theatre can be enormous. Stylistic innovation can be endless.

Brenton, 'Underground Explorations 1', p. 16

The Screens

Adaptation of Bernard Frechtman's translation of the play by Jean Genet.
First production: Bristol New Vic Studio, 20 Mar. 1973
  (dir. Walter Donohue).
Unpublished.

---

*A condensation of Genet's play for its British premiere, cutting
it down from a piece for thirty to forty actors playing 97 parts to
a three-hour version for six men and three women playing thirty
parts. Brenton's version was 'highly illegitimate' and involved a
'flagrant rewrite' of the last third of the play.*

Probably *The Screens* would work best performed as Genet originally
wanted it, in the open air. . . . In Bernard Frechtman's English translation
(adapted and pared down to a mere three hours' performance time by
Howard Brenton) we had to take Genet's contorted world-view, and there
were memorable scenes . . .

  Michael Anderson, 'Bristol', *Plays and Players*, June 1973, p. 64

The Bristol New Vic's abbreviated and updated version by Howard
Brenton . . . marks a major act of daring by the director, Walter Donohue,
but *The Screens* looks remote from the status of masterpiece . . . the play
is more an epic panorama on a theme of eastern fantasists . . . But given
the direct and political effect of the central colonial scenes . . . what
more survives?

  Nicholas de Jongh, 'The Screens', *The Guardian*, 22 March 1973

Jedefrau (Everywoman)

A free adaptation of Hugo von Hofmannsthal's *Jedermann (Everyman)*.
First production: 1974 Saltzburg Mozart Festival Fringe (dir. Robert
  Walker, translated into German by Dietmar Schönherr).
Unpublished.

---

*An anti-*Everyman, *parodying the traditional annual outdoor
revival of the play based on Max Reinhardt's production,*

including caricatures of Mozart and von Karajan. A group of women make a journey across modern Europe, eating male tourists along the way, and finally meeting with death on an autobahn.

The Life of Galileo

A translation of Brecht's play.
First production: Olivier Theatre, London, 13 Aug. 1980
   (dir. John Dexter, with Michael Gambon as Galileo).
Published: Methuen 1980, 1981.

Translating this play has cheered me up. That angry but circumspect, tough but sly attitude which Gramsci called 'pessimism of the intellect: optimism of the will' shines in its text. Its optimism is certainly not sentimental about reason's chances nor, indeed, about humanity's —

   THE LITTLE MONK: But won't the truth, if it is the truth, prevail — with us or without us?

   GALILEO: No. No no. As much of the truth will prevail that we make prevail.

And the intellect's pessimism says — this play is about truth betrayed. As the cold war in 1980 grips minds and distorts reality more fiercely than ever, that betrayal three hundred and fifty years ago is still with us. We have probably yet to live its full consequences under the mushroom clouds and the 'rain of fire'.

   And the will's optimism says — yes, but. Yes the play is about truth betrayed, but not quite. Not quite because a student of Galileo's, a boy in the first scene a man in the last, smuggles a book across a border to us, in the future. As in the play, so in life. The blood runs cold with fear when one thinks of the courage men and women find to carry truth over borders in our day. 'Unhappy the land that needs heroes'.

   One warning, if warning it be to you. There is a lot of loose talk about Brecht's 'Humanism', his 'Ambiguity'. Brecht was a humanist, for marxism is, to a marxist, the true humanism. Brecht was, like anyone with a sense of humour, a dab hand at irony and saying two or more things at once — 'Ambiguity'. But he was a communist. Oh yes, like it or not, he was a communist and a communist writer. Milton said he wrote *Paradise Lost* to 'Justify the ways of God to men'. Brecht, like a godless Milton of the twentieth century, one foxy eye on the great theme of the stars above, the other on the human mess below, set out to justify the ways of communism to men and women. The new science of Galileo's time is, in a mighty double meaning at the heart of the play, marxism now. I don't think it too far-fetched to see *The Life of Galileo* as Socialist Literature's Paradise Lost. It is a desperately timely play.

Brenton, 'Translator's Note', *The Life of Galileo*

I always disliked Brecht. To be frank, he frightened me. . . . I did *Galileo* — and this really is arrogant! — to find out what made that playwright tick. There's no better way of coming to terms with one of the dead and great, than — well, writing his play for him in your own language. *Galileo* overwhelmed me. It's a tremendous piece of writing. It's very, very fast. Line by line, scene by scene, he delivers vast amounts of information, wit, dramaturgy, at a dazzling speed. The only other mind that has that sense of dramatic speed is Shakespeare. He slams into the scenes, he delivers at once. He was breathtaking. *And* he was a communist, on humanity's side. It's interesting how many critics, Martin Esslin and so many others, have tried to assassinate his integrity, his talent, his conduct. But the revivals of his best plays keep on coming, even in these reactionary times.

Brenton, 'The Red Theatre under the Bed', p. 199-200

In an interview a couple of years ago Howard Brenton described himself as 'an anti-Brechtian'. Now here he is as the translator of . . . *Galileo* . . . a play whose central event, appropriately enough, is a recantation. . . . Mr. Brenton's version is mostly excellent. Its clarity is in line with the best aspects of the play. . . . Mr. Brenton suggests that Galileo's smuggled truths are a metaphor for Communism in our day. You can just as well equate them, if you start to think that way, with any other minority creed. . . . The play lives as a clean piece of story-telling, and as a celebration of genius.

Robert Cushman, 'Planetary Passions', *The Observer*, 17 Aug. 1980

A further objection against the National was raised concerning a programme description in the current production of Brecht's *Galileo* that the play was 'translated' by Howard Brenton. In fact Brenton's command of German is slight and he was heavily dependent upon a literal translation which was also commissioned but never mentioned. In fairness to John Russell Brown he did point out that Brenton only wanted the literal translation in order quickly to read through the original. Still, this raises a general question whether it is a service to literature to have distinguished foreign work translated in stages by different people and then consigned into the hands of someone whose appeal to theatre management is not his skill as a linguist but his reputation and box-office draw.

Christopher Edwards, "'Discovered Countries'" —
a Report on the Riverside Conference on Play Translation',
New Statesman, 12 Sept. 1980

I tried to write plays for these dead great writers in my own language. The rules I followed were (1) to get every reference and every image in the play into English, and (2) to get a rhythm equivalent to their sense of rhythm, without mucking it about. It is an attempt at 'an English text', which is why I called *Galileo* a 'translation', even though I didn't know German; whereas *Danton's Death* is a 'new version'.

Brenton, unpublished interview with Tony Mitchell, 1986

Danton's Death

A new version of Büchner's play from a translation by Jane Fry.
First production: Olivier Theatre, London, 21 Aug. 1982
  (dir. Peter Gill; with Brian Cox as Danton and John Normington as Robespierre).
Published: Methuen, 1982.

The play . . . is not (as is often said) a tragedy, but a comedy, a celebration of what we are: like all the great comedies it sings and celebrates, it does not judge. That is why those who rummage about in the play for the goodies and the baddies get so thoroughly lost. All the people in the play made the Revolution . . . They are all given their voice and they are all responsible. . . .

Once you cease to be frightened of the content of the play, in the same way that the characters are not frightened, the whole map of the socialist and communist tradition unfurls itself with all the marshes, volcanoes and precipices clearly marked.

Brenton, 'A Crazy Optimism', p. 26

Howard Brenton was right when . . . he condemned the false antithesis which results from the reduction of Büchner's passionate critique of the French Revolution into a facile tale of goodies and baddies. . . . What is so interesting about the study of Danton is not so much his humanity as his existential exhaustion. . . . This provided for continuing engagement with a production which, frankly, dragged and sagged over its three hours.

Christopher Edwards, 'History Play', *New Statesman*, 6 Aug. 1982

Howard Brenton's version, from a literal translation by Jane Fry, is robust. It keeps closely to the original German text, but Brenton has managed to infuse the script with a sense of power and urgency, nearly but not quite matching that of Büchner. The speeches, which can sometimes seem long in second-rate translations, flow with ease, clarity and sometimes a lyrical beauty. . . .

John Elsom, 'Danton's Death', *Plays and Players*, Sept. 1982

Conversations in Exile

Adapted from a translation of Brecht's dialogue by David Dollenmayer, commissioned by Foco Novo.
First production: in a double bill with Alfred Fagon's
   Four Hundred Pounds, performed by black actors, directed by
   Roland Rees in a touring production, 1983.
Published: in *Theater*, XVII, No. 2 (Spring 1986).

Two German emigrants in Finland, Kalle, a proletarian, and Zifel, a business man and physicist, drink beer, play billiards and discuss 15 different topics: Passports, Order, Fascism, the Weimar Republic, Heroism, Wealth, Pleasure, Humour, Communism, Thinking, Total War, Patriotism, Good Men and Survival. Agreeing that 'it's terrible to live in a country where there's no sense of humour' but 'even more terrible to live in a country where you need a sense of humour', they decide to start a cockroach extermination business together.

Conversations in Exile was written while Brecht was in Finland in 1937, himself an exile from Nazi Germany. . . . In its full form the piece is three-and-a-half, even four hours long, for it is not really a play. It is a philosophical dialogue between two aspects of Brecht's personality — the professional middle class man who wants to do well, to 'belong' and see the best in things (Ziffel) and the working class, alienated, foxy rebel whose doubt and cynicism are weapons of creativity (Kalle). . . .

The theme is survival in dark times. Brecht turns the characters this way and that, holding ideas up to the light for inspection: it's like a playwright's doodle which spreads into extraordinary and revealing shapes. . . . The episodes could be played in any order. It is a suspended meeting in a historical limbo, between two men whose names are certainly not the names they give each other and who may be lying through their teeth. They are ordinary men, in the process of being forced to become extraordinary. From that comes the piece's optimism, its 'devil may care' quality. Human transformation is in the air.

Brenton, 'The Best We Have, Alas', p. 7

f: Collaborations

Lay By

Two act play, written with Brian Clark, Trevor Griffiths, David Hare, Steven Poliakoff, Hugh Stoddart and Snoo Wilson.

First production: Edinburgh Festival, 24 Aug. 1971 (dir. Snoo Wilson), and subsequently at the Royal Court Theatre Upstairs.

Published: in *Plays and Players*, Nov. 1971, and Calder and Boyars, 1973.

Based on a newspaper report about a rape case involving fellatio in a van on the M4. Lesley, a model, and another girl pose for a hunchback porn photographer in the country; the fellatio takes place in the van, in the presence of the driver's mistress, a mother of five. A lawyer questions Lesley, who is unconcerned about the incident, and gets her to re-enact it. Despite the difficulty of establishing fellatio as rape, the van driver is sentenced to ten years in Brixton. Lesley, who is also revealed to be a heroin addict, is sent to Holloway prison where she has a baby. The final scene takes place in a hospital mortuary, where Lesley is taken after she attempts to perform an abortion on herself with knitting needles. The bodies of the three main characters are washed in blood, put into a dustbin, and made into jam.

It all began on a dreadful rainy afternoon when we were all lounging around the stage of the Royal Court. It was meant to be a writers' meeting — they're always disastrous kinds of meetings. David Hare said 'Why don't we just get to know a bit about what we're like as writers by writing a play together. Join me in the bar if you fancy it.' Seven of us did, and Trevor Griffiths had a press cutting about this terrible case on the M1. It was written by a liberal journalist, Ludovic Kennedy, and it tried to make sense of this event. We thought there was no sense in it — it was just ugly and terrible — and this sermonizing about it was just impossible. So we set out not to sermonize. It was an anarchic mess, the whole show. It was written in crayon, which was my idea, on huge sheets of wallpaper. The script was sellotaped together. Trevor Griffiths, Steven Poliakoff and I wrote the last 20 minutes as a total piss-take on that Kennedy sociological tone. . . . It was a protest against using a tragic and horrible event like that. To our amazement, it was taken seriously, whereas it was a blatant piss-take. So the show had no control over itself at all.

Brenton, unpublished interview with Tony Mitchell, 1986

Just in case anybody thinks this is the direction in which the theatre should be going (Andy Warhol-style deadpan confessional, the dramatist as ventriloquist), let me assert that *Lay By* was the most moronic rubbish I have yet seen on the London stage. Described as a play about 'people who do it in the road, their specialized tasks and subsequent arrests', it was worse, because visually less interesting, than a competent strip show. No greasy raincoats at the Royal Court, of course.

Derek Mahon, 'For Trendies', *The Listener*, 30 Sept. 1971

. . . I am more disturbed in another way while watching this show. In it there seems to be a strange sort of arrogance, a holier-than-thou attitude directed at the audience. The authors appear to be saying that only they are prepared to look at the events as they happen, and that the events themselves actually need this sort of exposure otherwise we shall avert our eyes and not see the significance of what happens in our society. . . . One cannot help but feel that there is a certain amount of self-congratulatory back patting on the part of the company and the authors, that they have had the guts and harboured the sense of duty to show the rest of us what happened. . . .

Chris Barlas, 'Lay By', *Plays and Players*, Nov. 1971, p. 48

A triumphant vindication of team drama, of a play created and welded together by seven writers . . . working by committee and in discussion.

Invading such fragile territory has its risks but the writers confront and overwhelm them. The play had a unifying style, a combination of verbal surrealism and documentary reportage . . . achieves its sharpest insights in its surrealistic comedy. . . . Its sustained view of exploitation and its courage in treating sex as indefatigably comic makes *Lay By* a major theatrical event. . . .

Nicholas de Jongh, 'Lay By',
The Guardian, 26 Aug. 1971

England's Ireland

A two act play, written with Tony Bicat, Brian Clark, David Edgar, Francis Fuchs, David Hare, and Snoo Wilson.
First production: by Shoot Theatre, at the Mickery Theatre, Amsterdam, September 1972 (dir. David Hare). Subsequently at the Roundhouse, London, 2 Oct. 1972, and in Glasgow, Lancaster, and Nottingham.
Unpublished.

A 'collision' of twenty scenes with songs attempting to bring home the 'stench' of the Irish troubles to English audiences. A brief history of British political involvement in Northern Ireland since the 1920s is followed by a presentation of the Loyalist viewpoint; the civil rights march of 1969 led by Bernadette Devlin; a television interview with an elderly British colonel in 1992, looking back on the army's involvement in Northern Ireland; an illustration of the absurdity of British military regulations about firing on civilians. Sean O'Christie, an IRA suspect, is tortured by British soldiers and consequently turned into a Provisional because of his ordeal, which is paralleled with Christ's passion. In the second act an Irish comic tells racist, anti-Irish jokes which turn into a Provisional tract; an Orange Lodge ceremony involving excrement takes place, followed by a UDA military exercise; a priest hears a Catholic woman's last confession, and a dialogue between Provisional and Official IRA members takes place. The play ends with 'stories to tell our children' in the form of grisly anecdotes about the Irish situation.

It was obvious that *England's Ireland* had to be written. It was obvious to all of us that none of us could write sufficiently on it by himself, being English. Therefore, we had to try and write it collectively. There is a case for it. It does mean that personal writing . . . goes to the wall. . . . So we went away and rented a house in Wales and wrote for eight days, by which time we'd produced a huge draft. The difficulty of the kind of writing it produces is that it makes its argument not by straight description, Brechtian display or slogan, but by a manipulation of dramatic temperature. . . .

The argument of the show is much clearer, in a sense, than it played for most people. But that's one of the effects of group writing. For instance, you can have an argument about the Orange Lodge and you then write the scene. The texture of the writing, the feel of it, reflects what is in fact a straight argument, a straight position. Now that's the drawback and also the strength. . . . I think it does provide a kind of expressionistic writing about public events, and that can be useful. I think it got nearer to the situation than many of the Irish plays we've seen recently.

Brenton, in 'Messages First', p. 29-30

It was largely a wasted opportunity by some bright and talented writers, who together ought to have produced something a lot better.

Jonathan Hammond, 'Fringe',
Plays and Players, Dec. 1972, p. 57

'Fair' must be distinguished from 'balanced', ie. halfway between right and wrong. This show is not 'balanced', . . . but it is 'fair', in that it does not, I think, wilfully suppress or distort evidence. . . . But fair men are at liberty to take sides . . . and their political sympathies are accordingly nearer Sinn Fein than any other faction. They don't take this position straightforwardly or without reservations, perhaps because they are, after all, seven and not one. . . .

Inevitably, there are omissions, concrete and philosophical: too little historical background. More importantly, perhaps, the authors never quite decide whether and how far violence may be a justifiable instrument of social change in Ireland. . . . Nevertheless, a vast amount of disparate matter — statistics, ideas, satire, song, theatrical dialogue — has been subsumed into something which the sustained concern of the writing and the disciplined energy of a good cast renders pretty coherent in feeling and tone: you should try to see it.

Benedict Nightingale, 'Fair Partisans',
New Statesman, 6 Oct. 1972

A Fart for Europe

One-hour show, written with David Edgar.
First production: Royal Court Theatre Upstairs, 18 Jan. 1973
    (dir. Chris Parr).
Unpublished.

Described ironically as 'a non-political event sponsored by the government'; a burlesque attacking the 1973 'Fanfare for Europe' celebrations. It begins with a parody of King Lear, *satirizing European high culture, and casting an anti-EEC Labour MP, bewildered at finding his views aligned with those of Enoch Powell's, in the role of Poor Tom. Nick and Peter, two trendy right-wing businessmen, use a map of Europe as a monopoly board to demonstrate that 'to keep Britain going, Britain must go'. They stage a mock Greek tragedy on the legend of Europa, and the play ends with a call for links with the European trades unions: 'Next time there's a miner's strike, make sure the lights go out all over Europe.'*

. . . combined perfectly the respective talents of its authors, Edgar's solid factual and statistical research and Brenton's weird, original theatrical imagination . . . certainly the most politically considerable contribution to the month.

Jonathan Hammond, 'Fringe', *Plays and Players*, March 1973

. . . gives us little but polemic. Nothing wrong with that, of course, provided it makes its case, which is that we must unite to liberate a Europe which is become the fiefdom of super-corporations. But it doesn't, and if it is to do so, it needs evidence more thorough and more sophisticated than the present splatter of Shakespearian parody, jibes at our cultural tradition, isolated facts, grim forebodings and bald statistics.

Benedict Nightingale, 'Baby Face', *New Statesman*, 19 Jan. 1973

Brassneck

A three-act play, written with David Hare.
First production: Nottingham Playhouse, 19 Sept. 1973

(dir. David Hare). *TV version:* transmitted on BBC1 'Play for Today',
22 May 1975 (dir. Mike Newell).
Published: Eyre Methuen, 1973.

*An old man, Alfred Bagley, comes to Stanton, a small town in
the Midlands, in 1945, and sets up a property business with fifty
pounds capital. He rises to the position of Master of the local
Masonic Lodge, and brings his nephew Roderick into his
business. After Alfred's death at his grand-niece's wedding,
Roderick, his poet wife and their two sons expand the business
into Europe, Asia and Africa. The local politicians eat out of
their hands until they run into bankruptcy and charges of
bribery. In the third act there is a reunion at the behest of
Sidney, Roderick's son, at his strip club 'The Lower Depths' in
the 1970s. Sidney persuades the family of the financial rewards
of importing Chinese heroin. The play ends with a toast to 'the
last days of capitalism'.*

We wanted a show about corruption in England, in a town like
Nottingham, but neither of us felt that independently we were wise
enough to write it, so we decided to write it together. . . . I feel it's
wholly my play, David feels it's wholly his, and yet it's neither of ours.
Yet it was. Both of us take full responsibility for it as a work. We tried to
keep it public — family struggles would always take place in public
rooms or spaces. . . .

> Brenton, 'Petrol Bombs . . .', p. 19

Brassneck is a mystical, not a realistic, play. If it were just another of
those family and social chronicles written by fortunate young men from
Cambridge to prove that the capitalism which has showered inestimable
privileges upon them is wicked, I might be interested in it; but I should
not be, as I am, passionately concerned about it.

Its extraordinary quality is its sense of the accurst. . . . Maeterlink
speaks somewhere of a third person being present in every dialogue in
his theatre, enigmatic and invisible, the unconscious but powerful idea
that the dramatist has of the universe, who gives to his plays their
resonance and reverberations. That person, not named, not embodied,
and of course not mentioned in the programme, is what makes
Brassneck so difficult properly to seize, and so impossible to escape
from.

> Harold Hobson, 'Bold as Brass', *Sunday Times*, 23 Sept. 1973

Though they may write in very different styles, Brenton and Hare do share a common view of the *content* of their plays. Hare's work has tended to reflect the self-enclosed and, finally, self-defeating society which surrounds middle class 'progressive' groups. . . . Equally Howard Brenton has a strong sense of public life in this country as an empty spectacle, a hoax perpetrated on the people by politicians of both the right and left. . . .

It's this treatment of the establishment from the inside looking out (rather than vice versa) which distinguished *Brassneck* from most of its agit-prop brothers.

Peter Ansorge, 'Nottingham', *Plays and Players*, Nov. 1973, p. 64

It it had a fault it was that it attempted too much. In throwing the whole case of rotten eggs at us it left us little time to examine a single one. Its characters, too, were sometimes just images of their decadent society. But it made glorious television. . . . The dialogue was icily apposite . . . in this sizzling indictment of our times. . . . We had Galsworthy and we had Priestley. But in the end, when the characters became symbolic and the setting stylized, the whole affair was Brechtian, too.

Leonard Buckley, 'Brassneck', *The Times*, 23 May 1975

Deeds

Two-act play, written with Trevor Griffiths, Ken Campbell, and David Hare.
First production: Nottingham Playhouse, 9 Mar. 1978
(dir. Richard Eyre).
Published: Plays and Players, May and June 1978.

Ken Deed, a builder's labourer from Moss Side, arrives home to discover his baby is dead and his wife, Mary, has disappeared. After the local hospital and the coroner can tell him only that the baby has died from dehydration, he sets out to discover the cause of death. An off-duty nurse informs him that chemicals in Nuzzles Milk Powder have caused the death, and Ken is subsequently jailed for assaulting a policeman in a supermarket with a can of the product. In prison he teaches himself to climb, and on his release he scales the building where the Nuzzles boardroom is situated. He eavesdrops on their plans for marketing their product in the Third World, harangues his drunken and beleaguered local Labour MP, confronts the Minister for Consumer Affairs — herself a mother of a young baby — and surprises the Nuzzles director in a bath with two naked women, forcing him to sign 'Murder' on the baby's death certificate. He is finally reunited with Mary, who is eight months pregnant, as he is trying to drown himself in a railway tanker wagon full of Nuzzles. The couple decide to call their new baby Geronimo or Boadicea, and Ken builds a cradle out of bricks and barbed wire.

It would be idle to pretend the play offers detailed argument and characterization. It is much more a product of the New Expressionism dealing with essences rather than psychological subtleties, panoramic views rather than private lives. Its weakness is that you feel that one phone call to a newspaper or TV company by its hero would have achieved everything he set out to do. . . . Its great theatrical strength is that it combines a single-minded purpose with a wide angled lens.

Michael Billington, 'Deeds', The Guardian, 10 March 1978

. . . a depressing unanimity, in the striking of the most timidly conformist left-wing attitudes. . . . Do you suppose they have ever spent half an hour in the company of anyone who disagreed with them? . . . There is only one part not beneath contempt.

Bernard Levin, *Sunday Times*, 12 March 1978

The authors are so burdened with their sense of the wickedness all round them that they can't focus on any particular example. Police corruption, unemployment, racial violence, every obvious and conceivable cause is taken up, and as a result the impressive strength of the beginning is dissipated.

Jeremy Treglown, 'Etc.', *New Statesman*, 17 Mar. 1978

The sum of the writing talent turns out to be less than what might have come from each writer alone, but it is revealing of all of them that what began as satirical entertainment evolved into a social comedy based on tragedy. It is obvious at times that the picaresque form is a convenience. The hero, Ken Deed, like his phonetic cousin, Candide, is transported from adventure to adventure while he tries to understand the reason for his suffering, but his exposure to different worlds . . . is a means to take in the writers' separate voices. The unanimity of their voices, however,

on the theme of social injustice, gives an impressive coherence to the
play not unlike the Jacobean plays from teams of authors.

Ned Chaillet, 'Deeds', *Plays and Players*, May 1978, p. 24

A Short Sharp Shock!

Two-act play, written in collaboration with Tony Howard.
First production: Theatre Royal, Stratford, East London, 21 June 1980
(dir. Robert Walker), transferring to Royal Court Theatre,
16 July 1980. Also by Sheffield University Theatre Workshop,
21 June 1980 (dir. John Bull and Louise Page).
Published: Thirteenth Night and A Short Sharp Shock! (Methuen
Theatrescript, 1981).

Originally entitled Ditch the Bitch, *but changed after feminist
objections,* A Short Sharp Shock!, *is about the attempts of a
'mad socialist extended family', the Stackers, who run a junk
shop of socialist memorabilia, to counter the Thatcher
government. The play begins with their celebration of the
victory of the Wilson Labour government in the 1974 election,
and follows it with the ghost of Airey Neave, who summons Sir
Alec Home and Lord Thorneycroft to find a successor to
Edward Heath as leader of the Conservative Party. They choose
Sir Keith Joseph, who fails to pass the test, and instead
Margaret Thatcher ushers in 'a new age of self-interest'. The
Stackers witness the 1979 general election which brings her to
power, and Pipkin, the Stackers' assistant, joins the
Conservative Party. Sir Keith Joseph meets the Alien, in the
form of Professor Milton Friedman whom explodes out of his
chest and preaches monetarism, and the 1979 Tory Party
Conference takes place in Blackpool, attended by Pipkin. In Act
Two, an Emergency Cabinet meeting is announced when the
Tory Wets want a U-turn. Jim Prior, who Thatcher describes as
'the only effective opposition in this country', and who is
suspected of communicating secretly with Heath, is summoned
by Willie Whitelaw. At the meeting, Margaret produces a bottle
of Milton Friedman's sperm, 'the milk of monetarism', which
she makes Prior drink. The Stacker family meanwhile discuss*

effective opposition tactics. Pipkin appears, disillusioned with the Tory Party and now pledged to Anarchism. Margaret eats some of Neave's ashes, and invites the British public to kiss her arse.

I thought that the audience — working class, labour and union activists bussed into the theatre — so wanted a belly laugh after the General Election, that they pretended *A Short Sharp Shock!* was better, and funnier, than it was. No harm in that, why not encourage the troops? But as a playwright with a pride in what I try to do, I was uneasy. By force of will the audience turned a dodgy play into a great night out. . . .

The fault with *A Short Sharp Shock!* was a classic playwriting mistake. It was in the hardest of epic forms, an 'A-B-A' twinning of two separate plots, to show each other off, meeting in a big final scene. . . . the two plots were a farcical, cartoonish, extreme knockabout presentation of Thatcher's cabinet, set against a gentler, affectionate presentation of a bizarre left-wing family a 'red Galsworthy saga' with the family going through every conceivable left-wing split and difficulty. The mistake was that the scabrous, belly-laugh farce of the cabinet scenes so worked the audience up that the quieter, more loving humour of the family was swamped. Crude farce blasted ironic humour off the stage. We should have written one or the other.

Brenton, 'Writing for Democratic Laughter', p. 11

The furore . . . has covered the play with a sacred armour that prevents either praise or condemnation from affecting its reputation. . . . It is essentially a mild and liberal criticism of the Government . . . it seems to tell a story but it never moves far from the style of a well-written university review. . . . It functions as a lampoon. . . . Its good humoured theatricality is not threatening.

Ned Chaillet, 'A Short Sharp Shock!',
The Times, 27 June 1980

Unluckily, both the voltage and wattage of *Shock* are disappointingly low. It is neither good Brenton nor rousing agitprop. . . . The leading grotesques are all played by women . . . The laughter they provoke is not, however very abundant or savage; and the lines thrust into their mouths are neither particularly inventive nor especially informative. . . . Perhaps the evening needs an injection of the tastelessness it has already, bewilderingly been charged with displaying.

Benedict Nightingale, 'Low Voltage',
New Statesman, 4 July 1980

Sleeping Policemen

Play in two parts, written with Tunde Ikoli, commissioned by
Foco Novo.

First production: by Foco Novo in Hemel Hempstead, 4 Oct. 1983, then
at the Royal Court Theatre Upstairs, 8 Nov. 1983 (dir. Roland Rees;
with Alfred Fagon as Bert).

Published: Methuen, 1984.

*Peckham, in South London, as seen through the eyes of six of its
inhabitants, presented first in a lengthy collage of isolated
soliloquies. Paul, a film editor, is prone to walking about in a
gorilla suit, and becomes a right-wing racist after his flat is
broken into and his compact disc player stolen. Bert is a
'ragged trousered poet' who walks his two dogs, War and
Peace, around the streets, and 'sees the citizens of Peckham as
a lost army'. Elizabeth is an eccentric poet, Lana an Irish
woman deserted by her husband and courted by the IRA, Dinah
a Labour Party member who persuades the other characters to
come to a local branch meeting about sleeping policemen, with
the result that Castella, a West Indian bus conductor, stands for
the local council. By the end of the play, the characters'
isolation has been broken, and they are all helping one another,
with the exception of Paul, who attacks Castella with an empty
whisky bottle, but is knocked to the ground by him, then slashes
Bert's neck with a razor, and makes arrangements to move to
Belsize Park.*

The brief for the two playwrights involved a series of monthly meetings
to discover the perimeters of the play, mutually to choose the six
characters around which their plays were to be based and cast, to take
part in workshops in the area with the actors, and then to depart
separately to write their plays, based on the same six characters and the
material unearthed in the workshop.

The playwrights had four weeks in which to write their plays. They
did not communicate during this period. Director and playwrights then
met, read the plays and commenced to intercut scenes and parts of
scenes. The intention was a schizophrenic view of character to represent
accurately the experience of six people within urban life. This afforded
the scope of different developments in character and even separate

responses to the same incident. It also provided the opportunity to change the gears between different parts of people's lives — in short to dispense with the usual distinction between subjective and objective reality.

It is a method which permits the fertility and richness of two imaginations, two methods of writing to countenance the same experience. Another version of collaboration.

Roland Rees, 'Director's Note', *Sleeping Policemen*, p. 7

We wrote our own plays — I did what I could in writing West Indian parts. What I thought I knew I included; what I didn't know I didn't have to write about, because God knows what Tunde was doing. I did what I could, in a complete play. He did the same for the white characters. We then met, and we had two different plays, with different incidents happening, and we agreed not to emulsify it into some kind of liberal stew. We intercut them, and that decided what the style was like. And it worked. The expression 'whereof I cannot speak thereof I must be silent' is a good rule of thumb, I think, for white writers writing black parts . . . we do not have the experience of being below in racial matters . . . we move bricks around from on top.

Brenton, Keynote Address,
Australian National Playwrights' Conference, May 1984

Buried inside the play is a calm, commonsense plea for mutual help . . . appearing in a network of positive relationships that gradually spin out like so many fragile life lines.

Irving Wardle, 'Sleeping Policemen',
The Times, 12 Nov. 1983

The result is like a radicalized, phantasmagoric *Under Milk Wood*. . . . Next time I pass through . . . Peckham I shall certainly look at the place with fresh eyes. . . . The play does quite effectively suggest that every block of council flats teems with eccentric human dramas.

Michael Billington, 'Sleeping Policemen',
The Guardian, 12 Nov. 1983

Pravda

'A Fleet Street Comedy'.
Two-act play written with David Hare.

First production: Olivier Theatre, London, 2 May 1985
   (dir. David Hare; with Anthony Hopkins as Lambert LeRoux).
Published: Methuen, 1985.

The play follows the fortunes of Andrew May, a reporter on The
Leicester Bystander, *and the South African media magnate and
sports promoter Lambert Le Roux, who buys* The Bystander *and
appoints Andrew as its editor. Le Roux then buys* The Daily
Tide, *'a ranting, nipple-ridden broadsheet' in London, and
enlists the help of an MP, Peter Quince, to acquire* The Daily
Victory, *'the only newspaper with England on its masthead. An
institution, like Buckingham Palace, the Tower of London, and
your two Houses of Parliament'. He sacks the* Victory's *editor,
Elliot Fruit-Norton, and replaces him with Andrew. Act Two
begins with Andrew winning the 'Golden Typing Finger' for
editor of the year. His wife Rebecca, daughter of the former
owner of* The Bystander, *comes in with a Ministry of Defence
document about a plutonium leak cover-up which Andrew is
about to publish in the* Victory *when Le Roux appears and sacks
him. Andrew and Rebecca sink the* Victory's *chief competitor,
the* Usurper, *with the repercussions of the nuclear story, and
consequently join forces with Fruit-Norton, Quince, and
Le Roux's personal assistant, Eaton Sylvester, to outbid Le Roux
for ownership of the* Usurper. *They publish 'revelations' about
Le Roux's personal life which prove to be bogus, and Le Roux
sues them for libel. The play ends at* The Daily Tide, *which
Le Roux amalgamates with the* Victory, *with Andrew as editor.*

Because collaborative writing means that you speak, often shout, each
line out, or scribble then try it on your fellow writer, who at once grins
or grimaces, and because we wanted to go on the attack against the sort
of writing Fleet Street passes off on its readers, we decided from the start
to make the play, if we could, a monstrously funny comic monument, set
up on the most prominent stage in the country. . . .

   The kind of comedy we tried to write is one, we hope, of *democratic
laughter.* The audience are invited to dissociate themselves from the tiny
clique of the ruling class paraded across the stage. In the behind-the-
scenes deals we dramatized and in the frightening and trivial values of
Le Roux's mind, our intention was to say to our audiences 'Why do we
put up with all this?' As a joke between ourselves, to keep our spirits up

during the writing, we said 'We're writing this play to stop people reading newspapers'. . . .

> Brenton, 'Writing for Democratic Laughter', p. 9, 11.

No such Jonsonian ton of bricks has yet descended on the Fourth Estate even if you go back to Jonson's own *Staple of News*. Unlike previous authors having their bit of fun with the foibles of newsmen while taking care not to rock the boat, these partners tackle the maladies of Fleet Street as they tackled local government corruption in *Brassneck*. They nail up their message in the main title: signifying truth but meaning lies, and they are out to give offence, rattle skeletons and give people like me a hard time in writing this notice.

> Irving Wardle, 'Pravda', *The Times*, 4 May 1985

It is neither a work-play like Wesker's *The Journalists* nor a debate on press freedoms like Stoppard's *Night and Day*. Instead it is a boisterous, swingeing, sometimes crude satire on the degradation of newspapers by overweening tycoons and the mayhem of mercantile capitalism; and it harks back to the same authors' *Brassneck* and even further to Jonsonian comedy of humours. . . .

One feels that Brenton and Hare, having unleashed this spider from the bottle, cannot entirely control him. Like Richard III, he takes over the play. . . .

Unlike vintage satire, the play doesn't really possess a moral positive: it is hard to deduce from the evidence what kind of Fleet Street the authors ideally envisage. But it is a highly entertaining and scabrously funny play. . . .

> Michael Billington, 'The Street of Sham',
> *The Guardian*, 3 May 1985

Hare-Brenton sometimes seem a bit patronizing to their audiences and, indeed, to the British public itself. In their gaudy world even upmarket newspapers succeed only if they emphasize sex, scandal, crime and sport, sport, sport. Yet let me not carp and cavil, because most of *Pravda* is still marvellously enjoyable, packed as it is both with gleeful scurrility and with a lively lay concern about the many and obvious limitations of Grub Street.

> Benedict Nightingale, 'Rough Beasts',
> *New Statesman*, 10 May 1985

Alas, *Pravda* . . . is a play that any journalist — even the editors of *The Sun* and *The Times*, whose papers, lightly disguised as *Tide* and *Victory*, are prominent in the play — could recommend to his aunts without a second's misgiving. . . .

The action, a succession of short scenes, resembles a series of clever revue sketches put on in a university. The authors perhaps did too much research; they are too up-to-the-minute. As at a university revue, the audience is distracted by allusion-spotting. . . . The pompous deposed 'Fruit-Norton' must be Sir William Rees-Mogg and the northern editor come south must be Mr. Harold Evans and 'Cliveden Whicker-Basket' must be Mr. Charles Douglas-Home, the present editor of *The Times*. (Apart from the way his trousers hang round his ankles, Le Roux alone bears no resemblance to any living Fleet Street figure, such as Mr. Rupert Murdoch.)

The high-jinks on stage, and the fun . . . obstruct any substantial intellectual examination of the nature of the press, as at present owned and conducted.

Michael Davie, 'Urban Fire',
Times Literary Supplement, 17 May 1985

Its focus on the defeat of truth by lies in newspaper journalism, comes out of a changed view of the Left by some (not all) of the original dramatists of the new political theatre. . . .The liberal is back at the centre of the action but it is not the extreme Right which obliterate him with power and charisma. . . . In the end this play, for all its farce, is making a serious proposition about the relation of media to truth today. What it says is there isn't one. . . . It's a depressing picture of political alignments very different from what's found in Howard Brenton's and David Hare's plays of the 1970s.

Tony Dunn, 'Truth About the Truth', *Plays and Players*,
June 1985, p. 18, 20

Poems

Notes from a Psychotic Journal, and Other Poems.
   Brighton: privately printed, 1969.

Sonnets of Love and Opposition, 74 poems.
   In *Sore Throats and Sonnets of Love and Opposition*
   (Methuen Theatrescript, 1979).

Nail Poems: 32 Haiku.
   Royal Shakespeare Company, 1981.

Howard Brenton's poems follow after ten years of plays, in
performance and in print, and at first sight they seem like a
new departure. The collection . . . has the kind of completeness
and individual authority associated with the traditional sonnet
sequence. Yet in two important respects Brenton's poems are at
least as organic to his dramatic purpose as those of Brecht and
Bond. First, . . . the poems are an attempt to chart his everyday
landscape, moral and physical, and the poems operate through
actual description more than universal images, so that the
sequence has something of the effect of a journal. . . .

The individual poems are just the length of a manageable
single process of argument (two ideas, for example, opposed
and then drawn to a conclusion), but Brenton has also found in
the sequence its potential as a most direct form of drama.

   Paul Merchant, 'The Theatre Poems of Bertolt Brecht,
   Edward Bond, and Howard Brenton', p. 51

The Theatre is a Dirty Place (1972)

The theatre is a dirty place. It's not a place for a rational analysis of society — it's there to bait our obsessions, ideas and public figures.

A really great outburst of nihilism like *Fruit* or the last act of *Lay By* is one of the most beautiful and positive things you can see on a stage. Like the scene with the dead in Genet's *The Screens*. Nihilism is the end of everything — the closing down of all possibilities. Frankie Howerd's act is based on it — it comes from the comic's personal sense of self-destruction. His comedy is all about failure. Ken Campbell has got a sure popular touch — sketch after sketch — however light — has this sense of nihilism and breakdown. . . . But an audience survives all these assaults and horrors — it survives. And the fact of survival, no matter how we may degenerate, is surely important in itself.

'Underground Explorations No. 1', p. 16-17

Clashing Styles (1973)

I do think that there is a critical battle to be fought about the styles which are acceptable within one play. Coherence within a play is not a matter of choosing to write in one style. That's just sameness, superficial neatness. Actual coherence means using many different styles, moulding them, a deliberate process of selection, in order to express that *whole* in a play. Shakespeare did this all the time — he could move from a comic to a savage scene with great freedom.

When writers like Charles Wood and Edward Bond attempt the same thing they get criticized by the reviewers. Variations in tone and method are taken to be signs of incompetence.

Disrupting the Spectacle', July 1973, p. 23

The Dirty Art of Playwriting (1973)

What made me a so-called fringe writer was not an idea that it was ideologically good to be underground. . . . It was the fact that I found poverty of means a great help. . . . The discipline of poverty, I think, tends to rub out the difficulties of style. Playwriting is a very dirty art, it's not pure. I distrust all purists in the theatre, because they're only talking about style. The only way I can write is to use comedy basically and write gags. That's how I developed into writing stuff that isn't merely comic or satiric. And also the conflict isn't played out on the stage; there's no dialectic on the stage. Everything on the stage is rigged, because you put it there or your fellow-artists did. The true dialectic happens between the audience you address and the play itself. I suppose it's a very basic fringe idea.

'Messages First', p. 25-6

Theatre is a Bear-Pit (1973)

Theatre is very much a bear-pit, very much a cruel entertainment. If you think of a politically foul play like John Galsworthy's *Strife*, and it always gets you by the throat, you realize what a filthy thing the theatre can be, what a distorting medium. . . . With a medium like that, you can only be — almost — a firework display and the audience does what it will with it. But I don't subscribe to the Stoppard stupidity about 'Oh well, the theatre's no use, anyway.' If it's no use, then get out. You don't want to piss about all your life. The best you can do is try and kick theatre nearer to the centre of public life

'Messages First', p. 31

The Failure of the Fringe (1975)

I think the fringe has failed. It's failure was that of the whole dream of an 'alternative culture' — of a notion that within society as it exists you can grow another way of life, which, like a beneficient and desirable cancer, will in the end grow throughout the western world, and change it. What happens is that the 'alternative society' gets hermetically sealed, and surrounded. A ghetto-like mentality develops. It is surrounded, and, in the end, strangled to death. Utopian generosity becomes paranoia as the world closes in. Naive gentleness goes to the wall, and Manson's murderousness replaces it. The drift from the loving drug scene in Amsterdam in the late sixties to the speed and wretchedness five years later illustrates the process. The truth is that there is only one society — that you can't escape the world you live in. Reality is remorseless. No one can leave. If you're going to change the world, well, there's only one set of tools, and they're bloody and stained but realistic. I mean communist tools. Not pleasant. If only the gentle, dreamy, alternative society *had* worked.

'Petrol Bombs through the Proscenium Arch', p. 10-11

Brecht and Epic Theatre, 1 (1975)

There is a lot of difficulty with playwriting in an epic style, which is very important to develop. An epic style which has nothing to do with Brecht. Bond has gone the furthest. . . .

First about Brecht: I'm an anti-Brechtian, a Left anti-Brechtian. I think his plays are museum pieces now and are messing up a lot of young theatre workers. Brecht's plays don't work, and are about the 'thirties and not about the 'seventies, and are now cocooned and unperformable. I've never seen one that worked. The best of his work is the most militant and in a sense the most unfair and vicious. I mean the early plays, particularly *The Mother*, which is the one with the most life in it, and *St. Joan of the Stockyards*. But I think Brecht's influence is wholly to the bad. I've never found it attractive. I've never found it coherent. Young actors, amongst whom Brecht has a huge influence, perform Brecht simplistically, in a bad sense, perhaps because in his plays the morals are pointed, but not proven; correct, perhaps, but not proven by action. They're not demonstrated on stage. This is particularly true of *The Caucasian Chalk Circle*, where, in fact, nothing is proved, nothing connects with the class structure — or an audience.

'Petrol Bombs . . . ', p. 13-14

May 1968 and the Real World (1975)

May '68 was crucial. It was a great watershed and directly affected me. . . . May '68 disinherited my generation in two ways. First, it destroyed any remaining affection for the official culture. The situationists showed how all of them, the dead greats, are corpses on our backs — Goethe, Beethoven — how gigantic the fraud is. But it also, secondly, destroyed the notions of personal freedom, freak out and drug culture, anarchist notions of spontaneous freedom, anarchist political action. And it failed. It was defeated. A generation dreaming of a beautiful utopia was kicked — awake and not dead. I've got to believe not kicked dead. May '68 gave me a desperation I still have.

'Petrol Bombs . . . ', p. 20

Non-Communication and Envy (1976)

There's a myth put about by certain writers that there's something called non-communication: well that doesn't happen. People are capable of making themselves very clear. There's another myth that says intelligence matters. Differences of intelligence levels between people are marginal. Plays often admire intelligence, that is you're invited to admire the intelligence of a figure on the stage. And that intelligence is in some way a precious thing. The theatre is often constructed on an envy basis: the audience is invited to envy the wealth, the wit or the intelligence of the people on the stage. That's the recipe, the basis of bourgeois comedy.

'Ronald Hayman talks to Howard Brenton', p. 58

Political Theatre (1978)

All plays, even the lightest comedies on Broadway and television sitcoms, are political. You're only labelled a 'political' or a 'committed' writer if you're on the left. For example, the political drive behind Tom Stoppard's or William Douglas-Home's plays is very strong, fiercely meant, but they're not labelled 'committed' because that drive is not coming from the left. 'Committed', 'political' — two heavy, lumpy adjectives. They're thrown at your work to put people off it!

Interview with Malcolm Hay and Philip Roberts, p. 135

Brecht and Epic Theatre, 2 (1978)

I'm not sure whether the big stage plays I've written since 1973 are pure epics. Measured against the Brechtian, received idea of an epic they are far from being 'pure epics'. But then the notion of a form in the theatre being pure I view with great suspicion. . . . I had these notions of an epic in mind: (1) a play that is many-scened, the short scenes choosing precise 'windows' in a story, (2) the 'windows' have to be authentic, to ring true, and (3) at the same time they must be part of an argument, one illustrating the other, progressing to a conclusion that is believable, in the simple sense of 'men and women would do that' and also be clear in intent, and (4) it is the message of a play that comes first.

Interview with Malcolm Hay and Philip Roberts, p. 139

Vanguardism and Socialism (1980)

Writers on the left have to be a vanguard. They have to provide survival kits for people who are active politically. That is how I've seen the work so far. Also their work has to be at the service of the working class. But in ways that are difficult to describe because you are not performing to the working class. Therefore you are addressing them to people who are a potentially political vanguard. And that is why the plays often have painful issues. Like Stalinism; what the party is; what violent action is; the actual reality of working-class life; working-class consciousness, which a lot of people on the left have to be told. . . .

Theatre doesn't actually argue politically, that is done in meetings and parties and unions. But the theatre can illuminate what matters in those political meetings. So they go hand in had. But theatre itself is not a political act — the political act is voting.

Stages of the Revolution, p. 196-7

A Final Fling (1984)

It's my opinion that we're having a great time in the theatre in Britain at the moment with writing. Not since Elizabethan times has there been so much of such quality, and we have bust into the theatre, got a new kind of epic play working in it, put our foot down, got to the centre — a big guerrilla-like action. But it's my firm opinion that it's a wonderful funeral. I think the theatre is dying, because in the end it's the theatre of a dying culture. It's a late capitalist form of entertainment that people like me are having a great deal of fun in, messing up in a great final fling. That doesn't mean that theatre will stop, because theatre's part of human activity. We set up theatres all the time — when you tell a joke to someone, or a lie — it's a human function. It's not that kind of theatre that will die, or transmute, or change into something else, as our societies crack.

Australian National Playwrights' Conference, May 1984

Democratic Laughter (1985)

True, belly-laughing comedy, 'human comedy', is often dismissed as 'cheap', only 'a good entertainment'. I've come to the conclusion that it's the hardest and highest form of playwriting. It's the theatrical equivalent of being able to draw the human body well, warts and all.

'Writing for Democratic Laughter', p. 11

A 'New Jacobean' (1986)

I'm one of the 'new Jacobean' writers. I want both 'high' and 'low' in actin in a play. The plays are often about power and suffering — people who wield power and people who suffer under it. To do that you need, as the Jacobeans needed, the freedom to write in different styles, to range widely. You need 'comic' scenes and 'serious' scenes. Not to make pretty patterns! But because that seems a true expression, to me, of what life is like — something serious is often played out in a series of farcical events. The trivial and the cataclysmic go hand in hand.

'The Red Theatre under the Bed', p. 198

Poli-lolli-tics (1986)

Because I have a Marxist view of the world, right-wing critics are forever labelling my plays 'political', which is, for them, a euphemism for 'preachy'. Conversely some critics on the left find the plays 'too ambiguous', which I take to be a euphemism for 'not preachy enough'. I do not win on the middle ground either, as it is social-democrats who really get riled by my plays, for some reason. Perhaps the plays remind them of the allegiances they have betrayed.

Preface to *Plays: One*, p. vii-viii

a: Primary Sources

Collections of Plays

Plays: One. London: Methuen, 1986. [*Christie in Love,
     Magnificence, The Churchill Play, Weapons of Happiness,
     Epsom Downs, Sore Throats*.]
Plays for the Poor Theatre. London: Eyre Methuen, 1980.
     [*The Saliva Milkshake, Christie in Love, Heads, Skinny
     Spew, Gum and Goo*.]

Articles and Essays

'Haiku for Margaretta D'Arcy on Her Rubbishing of My Play',
     New Statesman, 14 September 1979, p. 377. [16 Haiku
     defending *Sore Throats* against D'Arcy's accusations of
     misogyny, and replying to her views on socialism and the
     British in Northern Ireland.]
'Who Will Judge our Morality?', *New Statesman*, 2 Apr. 1982,
     p. 10. [Comments on the trial of *The Romans in Britain*,
     Brecht, libertarians, and moral campaigners.]
'A Crazy Optimism', *New Statesman*, 30 July 1982, p. 26-7.
     [Reflections on translating Büchner's *Danton's Death*.]
'Tea and 7Up as the Bombs Fall', *The Times*, 6 Aug. 1982.
     [Account of the three days he spent in West Beirut at the
     invitation of the Bertrand Russell Peace Foundation.]
'Writing for Democratic Laughter', *Drama*, No. 3 (1985),
     p. 9-11.[About political satire, comedy, and writing
     Pravda.]
'"The Best We Have, Alas": Note on Brecht', *Theater*,
     XVII, No. 2 (Spring 1986), p. 5-7. [Brecht as the greatest
     twentieth century playwright, but a disappointing model.]

Interviews

'Getting the Carp out of the Mud', *Plays and Players*,
     Nov. 1971. [Brenton, David Hare and Snoo Wilson
     interviewed by John Ford about *Lay By*.]
'Underground Explorations No. 1: Portable Playwrights',
     Plays and Players, Feb. 1972, p. 14-18. [Interview with
     Peter Ansorge about his work up to *Fruit*.]
'Underground Explorations No. 4: War Games',
     Plays and Players, May 1972, p. 14-17, 61. [Members of
     the Traverse Theatre Workshop talk to Peter Ansorge about
     working with Brenton on *Hitler Dances*.]
'Disrupt the Spectacle, the Obscene Parade: Bring it to a Halt',

Time Out, 22 June 1973. [Interview with Dusty Hughes about *Magnificence*.]

'Disrupting the Spectacle', *Plays and Players*, July 1973, p. 22, 23. [Interview with Peter Ansorge about *Magnificence* and *Measure for Measure*.]

'Messages First', *Gambit*, VI, No. 23 (1973), p. 24-32. [Interview with Jonathan Hammond about *Skinflicker*, *Measure for Measure*, *Fruit*, *Magnificence*, *Lay By*, *England's Ireland*, and the Fringe.]

'Hugh Hebert Interviews Howard Brenton', *The Guardian*, 9 May 1974. [About *The Churchill Play*.]

'Meet . . . Playwright for Today', *Observer Magazine*, 16 Nov. 1975. [Biographical interview with Robert Cushman.]

'Petrol Bombs Through the Proscenium Arch', *Theatre Quarterly*, V, No. 17 (1975), p. 4-20. [Extensive interview about all his work up to *Weapons of Happiness*, with Catherine Itzin and Simon Trussler. Reprinted in Simon Trussler, ed., *New Theatre Voices of the Seventies*, Methuen, 1981.]

'The Man Behind the Lyttelton's First New Play', *The Times*, 10 July 1976.

'Ronald Hayman Talks to Howard Brenton About His Work', *The New Review*, III, No. 29 (August 1976), p. 56-8. [About *Weapons of Happiness*, childhood, Cambridge, Portable Theatre and playwriting.]

'Howard Brenton: an Introduction' and 'Interview: Howard Brenton', *Performing Arts Journal*, III, No. 3 (Winter 1979), p. 132-41.

'How a Bitch was Ditched in the Name of Satire', *The Guardian*, 20 June 1980. [Brenton, Tony Howard and Robert Walker talk to Andrew Veitch about *A Short Sharp Shock!*]

'Still Slogging the Road to Utopia', *The Guardian*, 9 Sept. 1983. [Interview with Hugh Hebert about *The Genius*.]

'Howard Brenton: a Maverick Figure Finds Favour with the Mainstream', *Sydney Morning Herald*, 5 May 1984. [Interview with Alison Summers about *Thirteenth Night* and *The Romans in Britain*.]

'The Red Theatre under the Bed', Howard Brenton interviewed by Tony Mitchell, *New Theatre Quarterly*, III, No. 11 (August 1987), p. 195-201. [A wide-ranging discussion of all the plays from *Weapons of Happiness* to *Pravda*.]

b: Secondary Sources

Articles and Chapters in Books

Jonathan Hammond, 'Brenton', in James Vinson, ed., *Contemporary Dramatists* (London: St. James Press, 1973), p. 116-19.

Peter Ansorge, *Disrupting the Spectacle: Five Years of Experimental and Fringe Theatre in Britain* (London: Pitman, 1975), p. 1-10, 18-21, 48-51.

John Peter, 'Meet the Wild Bunch', *The Sunday Times,* 11 July 1976.

Albert Hunt, 'Theatre of Violence', *New Society,* 4 Nov. 1976, p. 261-2.

Oleg Kerensky, *The New British Drama: Fourteen Playwrights since Osborne and Pinter,* (N.Y.: Taplinger, 1977), p. 206-25.

Paul Merchant, 'The Theatre Poems of Bertolt Brecht, Edward Bond, and Howard Brenton', *Theatre Quarterly,* IX, No. 34 (Summer 1979), p. 49-51.

Ronald Hayman, *British Theatre Since 1955* (Oxford University Press, 1979), p. 92-7.

Catherine Itzin, *Stages in the Revolution: Political Theatre in Britain since 1968* (Methuen, 1980), p. 187-98.

Steve Grant, 'Voicing the Protest: the New Writers', in Sandy Craig, ed., *Dreams and Deconstructions: Alternative Theatre in Britain* (London: Amber Lane Press, 1980), p. 117-22.

Ben Cameron, 'Howard Brenton: the Privilege of Revolt', *Theater* XII, No. 2 (Spring 1981), p. 28-33.

Richard Beacham, 'Brenton Invades Britain: *The Romans in Britain* Controversy', *Theater* (Spring 1981), p. 34-7.

Bernard Weiner, 'The *Romans in Britain* Controversy', *The Drama Review,* XXV, No. 1 (March 1981), p. 57-68.

Philip Roberts, 'Howard Brenton's Romans', *Critical Quarterly,* XIII, No. 3 (1981), p. 5-23.

Benedict Nightingale, *Fifty Modern British Plays: a Reader's Guide* (London: Pan/Heinemann, 1982), p. 438-47. [On *The Churchill Play.*]

Roger Cornish, 'Howard Brenton', in Stanley Weintraub, ed., *British Dramatists Since World War II* (Detroit: Gale Research Co., 1982), p. 100-08

Rosemary Pountney, 'Brenton', in James Vinson, ed., *Contemporary Dramatists,* 3rd edition (New York: St. Martins Press, 1982), p. 117-19.

John Bull, *New British Political Dramatists* (London: Macmillan, 1984), p. 14-18, 28-59, 97-107, 204-209, 219-221.

Michael Poole, 'Lie Detector', *The Listener,* 8 March 1984, p. 30. [On *Desert of Lies.*]

Tony Mitchell, 'Crank with a Cause: the Plays of Howard Brenton',
  The Age Monthly Review (Melbourne, Sept. 1984), p. 7-8. [On *The
  Genius* and *Sleeping Policemen.*]
Donna Soto-Morettini, 'Disrupting the Spectacle: Brenton's
  Magnificence', *Theatre Journal*, March 1986, p. 82-95.
Roger Cornish and Violet Ketels, 'Howard Brenton', in *Landmarks of
  Modern British Drama: the Plays of the Seventies* (Methuen, 1986),
  p. 85-91.

Reference Sources
Tony Mitchell, 'Howard Brenton Checklist', *Theatrefacts*, Vol. II, No. 1
  (1975).